Latin Language Tests: Mark Schemes

Latin Language Tests
Mark Schemes

Ashley Carter

Bristol Classical Press

Published by Bristol Classical Press 2012

Bristol Classical Press, an imprint of Bloomsbury Publishing Plc

Bloomsbury Publishing Plc
50 Bedford Square
London WC1B 3DP
www.bloomsburyacademic.com

First published by Gerald Duckworth & Co. Ltd. 2011

ISBN: 978 1 85399 7525

A CIP catalogue record for this book is available from the British Library

Printed and bound by CPI Group (UK) Ltd, Croydon, CR0 4YY

Contents

Introduction

The mark schemes that follow all adhere to the patterns and logic of those used in the public examinations. Careful application of the schemes should therefore enable teachers to approximate to the standards likely to be applied by examiners.

It should be borne in mind, however, that in a live examination the mark scheme will be finalised only after a large number of scripts have been appraised in order to see how wide-ranging the candidates' responses are and how well each question has met its expectations. Only then does formal marking actually begin. The schemes in this book, of course, have not had the benefit of that preliminary appraisal; teachers should therefore feel free to adapt the schemes according to what they find their students have written, though without compromising the overall standard that each scheme maintains.

Part of this process of adaptation will inevitably involve deciding which of the almost infinite range of variations of expression are acceptable and which not. The principle here should be to reward the accurate rendering of the sense of the Latin; if this is achieved, the precise wording is relatively unimportant.

Another issue is the distinction between comprehension and translation. Generally comprehension questions do not call for a precise rendering of every word. The answers given in the mark schemes generally do take the form of a translation simply because this is the kind of answer that most students try to give. Often a response that moves away from the Latin to take a broader or deeper perspective on what is happening will deserve full marks, even if none of the points in the mark scheme is apparent. Here the teacher's judgement must be exercised. Conversely, for questions which ask for a response in the student's own words, an accurate translation should still be given full marks. It is worth noting that tenses are rarely important in comprehension responses; this is partly because many candidates like to use the primary sequence in their answers, even though the Latin passage is in historic sequence.

As a general principle, for comprehension responses one mark is allocated to each Latin word. There are, however, exceptions to this: prepositional phrases often carry only one mark; so too do phrases containing a glossed word. This approach varies a little according to how many marks are available overall, and to the level of demand to which the questions are pitched; thus in the final section some questions award only one mark for several items of Latin. Again, part of the standardisation process in live examinations is to reallocate marks from one word to another, to wherever the light of experience shows them to be most effective.

Where a word is enclosed in <> signs, it indicates that the word logically belongs inside a neighbouring phrase carrying a single mark. Words in brackets should be ignored in marking.

It should be noted that several methods are used for marking translation; please see the notes at the beginning of each section. Some of these schemes call for the scaling of marks: please see the appendices for scaling charts.

Section 1: Tests for WJEC Level 1 Core

In Level 1 core translations, each Latin word generally carries one mark. Exceptions are where a word is glossed or straightforward prepositional phrases. A word should only be given its mark if it is correct both syntactically and semantically.

Do remember that, because of constraints of space, there is room here for only one version of each Latin word or construction to be given. Usually this will be the most obvious one, i.e. the one most students are likely to produce. In many cases the version given will be the most appropriate or idiomatic one; teachers must decide where to draw the line for less appropriate or idiomatic versions. In live examinations the guiding principle is that idiomatic English is not required, although it is certainly appreciated; also, less appropriate lexical choices should be accepted unless the sense of the Latin is compromised.

1

1	daughter (1) of Clemens (1)	[2]
2	(her / their) son	[1]
3	B	[1]
4	I want (1) you (1) to come (1) with me (1) today (1)	[5]
5	A, C	[2]
6	never (before) (1) had he entered / visited (1) the baths (1)	[3]
7	(i) (her) father	[1]
	(ii) visit the baths	[1]
	(iii) surely (1) I can (1) (can't I = 2) come (with you) (1)	[3]
8	*non potes* (1) you can't / no (1)	[2]
9	(i) go (1) with her mother (1)	[2]
	(ii) he could (1) take / lead (1) only (1) young men (1) (into the baths) (direct speech OK)	[4]
10	soon (1) Septimus (1) and (his) father (1) happily (1) left / departed from (1) the house (1)	[6]
11	(i) a slave	[1]
	(ii) carrying (1) oil and strigils (1)	[2]
12	(i) many (1) other (1) citizens (1)	[3]
	(ii) the baths	[1]
	(iii) *maximae* (1) very big / enormous / the biggest (1)	[2]
13	B, C, F, H	[4]
14	(i) handed (1) clothes(1) to a / the slave (1)	[3]
	(ii) so that he could guard them (*vel sim.*)	[1]
15	they sat	[1]
16	(i) quickly (1) left (1)	[2]
	(ii) it was difficult (for him) to / he couldn't (1) stand the heat (1)	[2]
17	D	[1]
18	jumped (1) into the water (1)	[2]
19	at last (1) Clemens (1) said (1) to Septimus (1) now (1) we must (1) leave (1) your (1) mother (1) is expecting / waiting for (1) us (1)	[11]
20	they looked for (1) their clothes (1) they couldn't (1) see them (1) (they weren't there = 2) the slave (1) guarding them (1) was missing / gone / not there (1)	[7]
21	Clemens was (1) very (1) angry (1)	[3]
22	buy (1) new tunics (1)	[2]
23	Clemens (1) saw (1) his wife (1) and daughter (1)	[4]
24	what (1) are you (1) doing (1)	[3]
25	C	[1]
26	A, C	[2]
27	*pulcher* (1) beautiful (1)	[2]
28	(but) where (1) is the slave (1)	[2]
29	(i) I sent him (1) to the shop (1)	[2]
	(ii) (he was) even (1) more (1) angry (1)	[3]
		Total [100]

2

1 she lived (1) in a beautiful house (1) [2]
2 many (1) slaves (1) (and) slave-girls (1) [3]
3 (she was) a slave (1) (and a)girl (1) [2]
4 A, C, F [3]
5 often (1) they went (1) to the shops (1) and (1) did (1) many (1) other things (1) (together) [7]
6 (i) go (1) to school (1) with her brothers (1) [3]
(ii) she was a girl [1]
7 (i) *dives* [1]
(ii) one (1) of / from the slaves (1) (a slave = 2) to teach her (1) [3]
8 D [1]
9 once / one day (1) Helena (1) said (1) to her father (1) why (1) (does) Hyacinthus (1) not teach (1) Phoebe (1) with me (1) [9]
10 an educated slave (1) has (1) more value (1) (is worth more = 2) [3]
11 he loved (1) his daughter (1) [2]
12 B, C, E [3]
13 everything (which) (1) Hyacinthus (1) knew (1) [3]
14 she still / even now / also now (1) had to clean (1) the house (1) [3]
15 the rest of the slave-girls (1) had (1) to do (1) Phoebe's work (1) [4]
16 they (1) were (1) very angry (1) refused / didn't want (1) to work (1) [5]
17 C [1]
18 (i) in the garden [1]
(ii) sitting [1]
(iii) why (1) aren't you working / don't you work (1) [2]
(iv) he's angry [1]
19 (now) she can read (1) and write / count (1) her life (1) is worse than before (1)
/ now she is educated (2) she is dissatisfied (1) with menial work (1)
/ any similar argument; accept direct speech [4]
20 hurried (1) to her father (1) told him (1) what Phoebe (1) had said (1)[5]
21 (her) father (1) when / after (1) he heard (1) this (1) was (1) even (1) angrier (1) because (1) he didn't want (1) to have (1) idle slaves (1)[11]
22 (i) A – because she calls him *carissime* / holds his hand (*vel sim.*)
(accept any other letter if supported by strong argument) [1]
(ii) D [1]
23 (i) give her (1) better work (1) [2]
(ii) being cruel / cruelty [1]
24 (i) to win her father over / *vel sim.* [1]
(ii) he had no alternative / what else could he do [1]
25 (i) recited poems [1]
(ii) (when Helena's) father (1) was giving (1) dinner (1) to friends (1) [4]
26 (i) all (1) his friends (1) praised Phoebe / her (1) [3]
(ii) happy [1]

Total [100]

3

1	in a school (1) near (1) the middle (1) of the city (1)	[4]
2	dined (1) trained (1) slept (1)	[3]
3	*fortis* (1) brave / strong (1) *parvus* (1) small (1)	[4]
4	he ran (1) under the swords of his opponents (1) and killed them (1)	[3]
5	(i) defeated (1) many opponents (1)	[2]
	(ii) the citizens (1) loved him (1)	[2]
6	when (1) Musculus (1) walked / was walking (1) through / along the streets (1) of the city (1) (city streets = 2) men (1) (and) women (1) greeted (1) him (1)	[9]
7	giving / staging / presenting / putting on (1) a show (1)	[2]
8	A	[1]
9	always (1) he wanted (1) to fight (1)	[3]
10	B, D, E	[3]
11	*difficilis* (1) difficult (1)	[2]
12	often (1) he had watched (1) him (1) in the arena (1)	[4]
13	Musculus (1) although (1) he was (1) quicker (1) than (1) Scorpus (1) could not (1) defeat (1) him (1)	[9]
14	(i) (Scorpus) was tired	[1]
	(ii) he knocked the sword (1) from his hand (1)	[2]
15	D	[1]
16	C	[1]
17	he held his sword (1) to his throat (1)	[2]
18	kill him	[1]
19	(i) to see if they wanted Musculus to live or die (*vel sim.*)	[1]
	(ii) they didn't want (1) him to die (1) / they wanted (1) him to live (1)	[2]
20	B, D, E	[3]
21	(i) happy (1) sad (1)	[2]
	(ii) (happy because) he was (still) alive (1) (sad because) Scorpus had beaten him (1)	[2]
22	a noblewoman (1) came (1) to the school (1)	[3]
23	what (1) do you want (1) madam / mistress (1) said (1) the slave (1) who (1) stood (1) at the door (1)	[8]
24	give (1) a gift (1) to Musculus (1)	[3]
25	led (1) the woman (1) to Musculus' cell / room (1)	[3]
26	I want (1) to buy you (1)	[2]
27	A, D, E	[3]
28	he was only qualified (1) to be a gladiator (1) / *vel sim.*	[2]
29	I want (1) to give (1) you (1) freedom (1)	[4]
30	take charge of the slaves (1) <all> (1) in her house (1)	[3]
		Total [100]

4a

1	(they were) friends (1) they lived (1) in neighbouring houses (1)	[3]
2	a large river	[1]
3	B, D, E, H	[4]
4	(i) looked at (1) the ships (1) gladly (1)	[3]
	(ii) the sailors (1) often threw them (1) small (1) gifts (1)	[4]
5	A, D, E	[3]
6	two (1) huge (1) men (1) jumped down onto the bank (1) (and) dragged (1) the boys (1) onto the ship (1)	[7]
7	(i) *fortiter* (1) bravely (1)	[2]
	(ii) B	[1]
8	soon (1) the boys (1) were (1) in chains (1) they had seen (1) <never> (1) crueller (1) men (1)	[8]
9	(i) what (1) do you want (1) why (1) have you captured us (1)	[4]
	(ii) free them / us (1) at once (1)	[2]
10	C	[1]
11	A (*nos*) = *vos* (1) B (*sumus*) = *estis* (1) C (*piratae*) = *servi* (1)	[3]
12	the citizens (1) (always) gave the pirates (1) much (1) money (1) when they sold (1) them (1) slaves (1)	[7]
13	they could (1) receive (1) a very great / the greatest (1) price (1) because they were (1) brave boys (1)	[6]
14	A	[1]
15	*perterriti* (1) terrified / scared (1)	[2]
16	when (1) they looked round (1) they saw (1) ten (1) boys (1) (and) a few (1) girls (1) sitting (1) nearby (1)	[9]
17	they were (1) in chains (1) they all (1) were afraid (1)	[4]
18	(i) a dog	[1]
	(ii) went (1) with his master (1)	[2]
19	when (1) the men (1) captured (1) (his) master (1) (and) his (1) friend (1) the dog barked (1) and (1) attacked (1) the men (1)	[10]
20	they cruelly (1) drove the dog away (1)	[2]
21	B, C, E	[3]
22	be quiet	[1]
23	(*tamen*) *non tacebat*	[1]
24	Crispus approached the dog (1) the dog ran to the door (1) the dog sat, looking at Crispus (1) Crispus came to the door (1) the dog ran into the street (1)	[5]
		Total [100]

4b

1	boys	[1]
2	left (1) their homes (1) (and) gone (1) to the river (1) near the city (1)	[5]
3	*perterriti* (1) terrified / frightened (1)	[2]
4	B, C, F	[3]
5	brave (1) faithful (1) (had) led Crispus (1) to the river (1)	[4]
6	standing (1) on the (river) bank (1)	[2]
7	Crispus (1) although (1) he was (1) angry (1) because (1) Fidus (1) had led (1) him (1) from the house / home (1) looked round (1)	[10]
8	he saw (1) Marcus' bulla (1)	[2]
9	the deaths (1) of the boys (1) (that the boys were dead = 2)	[2]
10	B, C, E, H, J	[5]
11	D	[1]
12	kidnapped many (1) citizens (1) for many years (1)	[3]
13	he hurried (1) to (his) friend (1) who (1) had (1) a large (1) (and) fast (1) ship(1)	[7]
14	(i) on his ship	[1]
	(ii) preparing to sail	[1]
	(iii) many sailors (1) were working (1) on the ship (1)	[3]
15	(i) relate / tell (1) what / that which (1) had happened (1)	[3]
	(ii) ordered the sailors (1) to set sail (1)	[2]
16	(i) down-river	[1]
	(ii) the other ship	[1]
	(iii) fleeing (1) quickly (1)	[2]
17	however / but (1) the ship (1) of Crispus (1) and his friend (1) was (1) quicker (1) than (1) the other (1)	[8]
18	B	[1]
19	B, C, F, H	[4]
20	drew their swords (1) prepared (1) to fight (1)	[3]
21	the sailors (1) soon (1) defeated the pirates (1)	[3]
22	Sextus (1) and Marcus (1) (and) the rest of the prisoners (1) were (1) very (1) happy (1) because (1) Crispus (1) (and) his friend (1) had freed (1) them (1)	[11]
23	walked (1) near the river (1) alone (1)	[3]
24	(i) gave (1) Crispus and his friend (1) a large reward (1)	[3]
	(ii) they had freed (1) so many boys (1) and girls (1)	[3]
		Total [100]

5

1	he was (1) a priest (1)	[2]
2	(i) many worshipped her / very	[1]
	(ii) she promised (1) (another) life (1) after death (1)	[3]
3	Octavius (1) was (1) now / already (1) happy (1) because (1) spring was approaching (1)	[6]
4	leading a procession (1) through the middle (1) of the city (1)	[3]
5	A, D	[2]
6	six	[1]
7	throwing flowers (1) at the feet of the priests (1)	[2]
8	it went / made its way (1) slowly (1) to the forum (1)	[3]
9	the priests (1) as soon as (1) they came (1) to the middle of the forum (1) placed (1) the statue (1) on the ground (1)	[7]
10	(i) approached (1) the statue (1) carried (1) gifts (1)	[4]
	(ii) they wanted the favour (1) of the goddess (1)	[2]
11	(i) A	[1]
	(ii) good fortune (1) (very) much corn (1)	[2]
12	(i) reply (1) on behalf of the goddess (1)	[2]
	(ii) (he was) the leader of the priests	[1]
13	B, C, E, H	[4]
14	all (1) the citizens (1) were (1) very (1) happy (1)	[5]
15	(i) angry	[1]
	(ii) (he was) a Christian (1) he didn't want (1) to see (1) other (1) gods (1)	[5]
16	D	[1]
17	suddenly (1) Peter (1) ran (1) among the leaders (1)	[4]
18	(i) she is not (1) a goddess (1)	[2]
	(ii) he alone (1) can (1) save you (1)	[3]
19	worship Christ (1) not Isis (1)	[2]
20	A, C, F	[3]
21	*optima* (1) excellent / very good / the best (1)	[2]
22	C	[1]
23	we don't want (1) to hear (1) about (1) your god (1)	[4]
24	I curse (1) you all (1) Christ must (1) punish you (1)	[4]
25	the priests seized him (1) and dragged him to prison (1)	[2]
26	(i) a large storm	[1]
	(ii) after a few days	[1]
	(iii) it destroyed (1) fields and houses (1) killed (1) many citizens (1)	[4]
27	*risit* (1) laughed / smiled (1)	[2]
28	my god (1) punished you (1)	[2]
29	(i) Christ	[1]
	(ii) very cruel	[1]
	(iii) he had punished the city / destroyed houses / *vel sim.*	[1]
30	A	[1]
31	he was executed / handed over to the executioners	[1]

6

1 (in) many (1) cities (1) [2]

2 A, D, E [3]

3 the Romans (1) because (1) they wanted (1) always (1) to buy (1) slaves (1) were ready (1) to give (1) much (1) money (1) [10]

4 *divitissimus* (1) very rich (1) [2]

5 (i) (those who) could (1) read (1) [2]
  (ii) happy *vel sim.* [1]
  (iii) when selling (1) a beautiful (1) slave-girl (1) [3]

6 she was among (1) the slave-girls (1) Labrax was selling (1) [3]

7 Aoife (1) had been (1) a noblewoman (1) who (1) had lived (1) in Gaul (1) [6]

8 B, C, E [3]

9 (i) to buy (1) the best (1) women (1) and girls (1) [4]
  (ii) he had (1) much (1) money (1) [3]

10 now / already (1) Aoife (1) was standing (1) in the forum (1) of Rome (1) awaiting / expecting (1) a new (1) master (1) [8]

11 bought her [1]

12 C [1]

13 but (1) among (1) his (1) slave-girls (1) none (1) was (1) more beautiful (1) than (1) Aoife (1) [9]

14 Aoife (1) understood (1) everything (1) he said (1) [4]

15 (i) to see if she could also read / *vel sim.* [1]
  (ii) read out the words (1) easily (1) [2]

16 invited friends (1) to dinner (1) [2]

17 to bring in / serve (1) the food (1) [2]

18 (i) (because) Lepidus had a beautiful slave-girl / *vel sim.* [1]
  (ii) (because) he owned her / she was only a slave / she had no rights / Rome was male-dominated / *vel sim.* [1]

19 to recite poems [1]

20 (i) a friend (1) of Lepidus (1) [2]
  (ii) Aoife [1]
  (iii) come here [1]
  (iv) kiss her [1]

21 Aoife was angry (1) the man was very angry (1) [2]

22 (i) you must (1) now (1) punish her (1) [3]
  (ii) do it / punish her (1) tomorrow (1) [2]

23 B [1]

24 hurried (1) to him (1) [2]

25 why (1) did you refuse (1) to obey my friend (1) yesterday (1) [4]

26 Aoife saw herself as a noblewoman (1) Lepidus as a slave (1) [2]

27 she accepted that she was formally a slave (1) / *vel sim.*
  she still saw herself as the daughter of a king (1) / *vel sim.*
  she refused to compromise that view (1) / *vel sim.* [3]

28 he was astonished / accepted her views / respected her / *vel sim.* [1]

7a

1	large (1) in the city (1)	[2]
2	wife	[1]
3	(i) a country house	[1]
	(ii) he was rich	[1]
4	B, C	[2]
5	in the middle (1) of the mountains (1)	[2]
6	Severus (1) went (1) not (1) often (1) to the country house (1) because (1) he was working (1) always (1) in the city (1)	[9]
7	the wife (1) of Severus (1)	[2]
8	in the mountains (1) the air was (1) always (1) pleasanter (1) than (1) in the city (1)	[6]
9	but (1) she did not want (1) to stay (1) there (1) alone (1)	[5]
10	he visited the house (1) rarely (1)	[2]
11	C	[1]
12	he supervised (1) many (1) slaves (1) in the house (1)	[4]
13	cleaned the house (1) worked in the fields (1)	[2]
14	put up with (1) the heat (1) in the city (1) (any longer)	[3]
15	Livia (1) as soon as (1) her husband (1) returned (1) to the house (1) said (1) I want (1) to go (1) to house (1) <our> (1)	[10]
16	D	[1]
17	A, D, F, G	[4]
18	(i) go (1) alone (1) to the house (1)	[3]
	(ii) stay here / there / in the city	[1]
	(iii) come (1) later (1)	[2]
19	Livia (1) left (1) quickly (1) with (1) two (1) slaves (1)	[6]
20	three (1) days (1)	[2]
21	(i) no (1) slave (1) had brought (1) him (1) a letter (1)	[5]
	(ii) that Livia was coming / *vel sim.*	[1]
22	he (secretly) loved (1) his mistress / Livia (1)	[2]
23	(i) have dinner (1) in the dining room (1)	[2]
	(ii) he was a slave	[1]
	(iii) bring (1) him (1) food (1)	[3]
24	A, C	[2]
25	(i) *benigna*	[1]
	(ii) she did not want (1) to order (1) him (1) to dine (1) with the rest of the slaves (1) in the kitchen (1)	[6]
26	(i) dine alone	[1]
	(ii) Livia (1) and Sparax (1) dined together (1)	[3]
	(iii) (wise) because she respected Sparax / *vel sim.* (foolish) because she was treating him like a free man / *vel sim.*	[1]
		Total [100]

7b

1 lived (1) worked (1) [2]

2 C [1]

3 dined with Sparax [1]

4 A, C, E [3]

5 invited him (1) to dinner (1) [2]

6 according to the law (1) she had freed him / he was free (1) [2]

7 astonished (1) angry (1) feared (1) her husband (1) [4]

8 (i) don't (1) report (1) this (1) to husband (1) <my> (1) [5]

(ii) she was afraid of her husband / she wanted to hide the truth / she had been foolish / *vel sim.* [1]

9 yes [1]

10 but (1) you must / ought to (1) give (1) me (1) money (1) now (1) [6]

11 his former life [1]

12 B, D, F, G [4]

13 (i) Livia's husband / Severus (1) bought him (1) he gave him (1) this work (1) [4]

(ii) (because) Sparax / he (1) was accustomed (1) to lead (1) men (1) [4]

(iii) being a farm manager [1]

(iv) yes [1]

14 (i) walked (1) with him (1) [2]

(ii) when he was inspecting (1) the slaves (1) [2]

(iii) go / travel / make her way (1) to the town (1) <nearest> (1) [3]

15 soon (1) they were (1) like (1) a wife (1) and husband (1) because (1) they did / were doing (1) everything together (1) [8]

16 (i) when they returned (1) from the city (1) (to the house) [2]

(ii) Severus (1) was waiting for them (1) [2]

17 he had finished his work (1) he wanted (1) to see (1) his wife (1) [4]

18 A [1]

19 (i) *iratissimus* (1) very / most (1) angry (1) [3]

(ii) questioned slaves (1) <other> (1) [2]

(iii) their / his wife's and Sparax's (1) friendship (1) [2]

20 A, C, F [3]

21 she felt guilty / she was upset / she upset Severus / *vel sim.* [1]

22 Sparax is (1) now a freedman (1) [2]

23 (i) even (1) angrier (1) [2]

(ii) A [1]

24 why (1) did you do (1) that (1) surely <not> (1) you are (1) stupid (1) Severus (1) asked (1) [8]

25 (i) she loved Sparax (1) she did not love Severus (1) [2]

(ii) her husband worked (1) always (1) she saw him (1) never (1) [4]

26 B, D, E [3]

Total [100]

8

1	B	[1]
2	he was (a) handsome / beautiful (1) young man (1) he lived (1) in the house next door (1)	[4]
3	Helen's father was a nobleman (1) Julius' father was poor (1)	[2]
4	And so (1) Helena's (1) father (1) refused (1) even (1) to greet (1) the father (1) of Julius (1)	[8]
5	A,D,E	[3]
6	(i) he went (1) with his friends (1) to the sportsground (1) near (1) the middle of (1) the city (1)	[6]
	(ii) she stood (1) near (1) the gate of the sportsground(1) waiting for (1) him (1)	[5]
7	(i) as soon as (1) he saw this (1)	[2]
	(ii) greet (1) the young man / Julius (1)	[2]
8	you ought (1) to have (1) a better (1) husband (1) than (1) him (1)	[6]
9	she wanted to obey her father (1) but she couldn't stop loving Julius (1) (Allow shorter versions.)	[2]
10	B,C	[2]
11	(i) astonished (1) glad (1)	[2]
	(ii) it had pleased him (1) for a long time (1) to look at (1) Helena (1)	[4]
12	for (1) Helena (1) was (1) more beautiful (1) than (1) all (1) the other (1) girls (1) who (1) lived (1) in the city (1)	[11]
13	(i) when he was walking (1) through the streets (1) of the city (1)	[3]
	(ii) to look for Helena	[1]
	(iii) she loved Julius / wanted to see Julius	[1]
14	they loved each other (1) equally (1) (*vel sim.*)	[2]
15	how to show (1) their love (1)	[2]
16	invite (1) Julius (1) into her house (1) enter (1) his (1) house (1)	[6]
17	A,D	[2]
18	(i) *desperans*	[1]
	(ii) eat (1) food (1)	[2]
	(iii) she was desperate / to persuade her father to relent / *sim.*	[1]
19	(i) either answer + any sensible argument	[1]
	(ii) *anxii*	[1]
	(iii) why (1) do you not (1) eat (1) dinner (1)	[4]
	(iv) die	[1]
20	(i) she loved / I love (1) Julius (1)	[2]
	(ii) *crudeles* (1) cruel (1)	[2]
	(iii) D	[1]
	(iv) live	[1]
21	fled (1) from the house (1) in tears (1)	[3]
22	accept (1) their love (1)	[2]
23	C	[1]
		Total [100]

Section 2: Tests for Level 1 Additional

Translations in this section are marked differently from those in the previous section. Here each inflected Latin word generally carries two marks: one for the meaning and one for the ending. Each of these two marks can be earned independently of the other. The ending mark generally embraces not only the correct case and number (for nouns), or person, number, tense, voice and mood (for verbs), but also the correct syntactical relationship with other key words. Thus, *amicos* would only be given its second mark if it were made the plural object of the correct verb.

The ending mark for adjectives is for agreement only, and so the mark should be given even if the case or number is wrong, because the noun will lose its ending mark for either of these errors; to withhold the mark for the adjective as well would be to penalise the same error twice.

A comparative or superlative adjective usually carries three marks. These are for the meaning, the degree of comparison and the agreement respectively.

Where a Latin word has already appeared earlier in the passage, there will be no mark for meaning (otherwise the same error would be penalised two or more times). Glossed words carry no mark for meaning. Prepositional phrases usually carry only one mark. Occasionally, usually when there is a shortage of marks, an inflected word will carry only one mark; to earn this mark both the meaning and the syntactical relationship must be correct. A small number of unimportant words sometimes do not carry a mark at all (typically *et* and occasionally *sed*). Where an italicised word carries a mark, this will be purely for the ending.

Some passages will appear to be marked more generously than others. This is because they contain a greater number of glossed words, or there is more repetition of words. Either situation leads to the need for fewer marks, and so enables elements to be given marks that otherwise would not be able to carry them. This type of variation, which is likely to generate higher marks, is taken into account in live examinations at the Award stage.

This type of mark scheme is very accurate in rewarding candidates precisely for what they know and understand. Its main drawback is that it is laborious to apply. It also tends to reward weaker candidates for showing some grasp of endings without a corresponding knowledge of vocabulary.

1

1 1 1 1 1 1 1 1 8
Caelius looked *round* the garden; he was looking for his son.

1 11 1 1 1 1 1 1 1 10
His son was *Quartus*. *Caelius* could not see *Quartus*.

1 1 1 1 1 1 1 1 1 1 10
He was angry, because he wanted to send *his son* to the shop,

1 11 1 1 1 1 1 1 1 10
for all the slaves had gone out already with his wife;

1 1 1 11 1 1 11 9
and so there was *no one* else who *could* go *to the shop*.

1 1 1 1 1 1 1 1 1 9
Caelius_himself remained in the house, waiting for a friend.

1 1 1 1 1 5
*Caelius want*ed to give *wine* to *his friend*,

1 11 1 4
but *there was* no *wine in the house*.

1 1 1 1 1 5
It was *necessary* for *Quartus* to fetch *wine*.

1 1 1 1 1 1 1 1 1 9
'*Quartus*!' shouted *Caelius*, 'where are you? Come *here* at once!'

1 1 1 1 1 1 1 1 1 1 1 11
His son did *not* reply. *Caelius* was even *angri*er. Then *his friend* arrived.

1 1 1 1 4
His friend, as soon as he had greeted *Caelius*,

1 1 1 1 1 1 1 1 1 9
said, 'I saw *your son* walking in the street.'

1 11 1 1 1 1 1 1 1 1 11
'What?' *Caelius* said; 'the boy is *very bad*. He ought to be *in the house*.'

1 1 1 1 1 1 1 7
Caelius, after he had hurried from *the house*, caught sight of *his son*.

1 1 1 1 1 1 6
'*Quartus*,' he *shout*ed, 'return quickly into *the house*!

1 1 1 1 1 1 6
I *want* to *punish* you, because you were not *able to go to the shop*.

1 1 2
Where were you?'

1 1 1 1 1 1 11 1 9
'*But* father,' *replied the boy*, 'mother sent me *to the shop*.

1 1 1 1 1 1 6
Here is the wine that *mother* asked for.' *His father* was *astonished*.

Total mark: 150/3 = [50]

2

1 1 11 1 1 1 1 1 1 1 11
Once *Septimus* said to his father: 'Why do we live in_*Britain*?

1 1 1 1 4
We are *Romans*.'

1 1 1 1 1 1 1 1 1 1 1 1 1 1 14
His father smiled. 'It is difficult for me to relate everything,' he replied.

1 1 11 1 1 1 1 1 1 1 1 1 1 14
'When I was a boy, I *lived* in the city of *Rome* with my mother and *father*.

11 1 11 1 6
My *father* was a *commander*.

1 1 1 1 1 1 1 7
After *Boudica* killed many *Romans here*,

1 11 1 1 1 1 7
the emperor sent a new *legion* to *Britain*.

1 1 11 11 1 1 1 1 10
My father led that *legion* for a few *years*.

1 1 1 1 1 1 1 11 1 10
My mother *and* I came to this *city* with_*my father*.

1 1 1 1 1 1 1 7
Then, because there was *a fort* near *the city*,

1 1 1 3
we *lived* in_*the commanding officer's house*.

1 1 1 1 4
Every day I saw *soldiers*.

1 1 1 1 1 1 1 7
When *father* returned to_*Italy*, I *joined the army*.

1 1 1 1 1 1 11 1 1 1 11
I wanted to stay in_*Britain*, because all my friends *were here*.

1 1 1 1 4
My legion was here in_*the city*.'

1 1 1 1 11 1 1 8
Septimus, when he heard this, *was astonished*.

1 1 1 1 1 1 6
'Surely you *were* not *a soldier*? I did *not know* that.'

1 1 2
'*Yes*,' *his father replied*.

1 1 1 1 1 1 1 11 1 10
'Then, when I left *the army*, I caught sight of your *mother*.

1 11 1 1 5
After_years <two>, you *appeared*.'

Total mark: 150/3 = [50]

3

1 1 1 1 4
Flavius was standing in_*the main room*.

1 1 1 11 1 6
Suddenly a slave ran into_*the main room*.

1 1 1 1 1 1 1 1 8
'Master! *master*!' shouted *the slave*. 'What is it?'

1 1 1 1 1 1 1 1 1 1 1 1 12
'A man is *standing* at the door. *The man* wants to say *something* to you.'

1 1 11 1 1 1 1 8
'Who is that *man*?' 'He *is a senator. His name is Scipio.*'

11 1 1 11 1 1 1 1 1 11
Flavius was *anxious*; for no *senator* had come to the house *before*;

1 1 1 1 11 6
Scipio was also a very *well-known* man.

1 1 11 1 5
After *the slave* led *the senator into the main room*,

1 1 1 1 11 1 7
Flavius ordered the slave to bring him *wine*.

1 1 1 11 1 1 7
'*Hello*, *senator*,' he said. 'What do you want?'

1 1 1 11 1 1 7
'Surely you have many shops?'

1 1 1 1 1 1 6
'*Yes*,' replied *Flavius*, who *had* ten *shops*.

1 1 11 1 1 1 7
'I *want* to *buy* one. *How much* money do you *want*?'

1 1 1 1 1 5
Flavius, because he did not want to *sell a shop*,

1 1 11 1 1 1 1 — 8
asked for more *money* than *was* reasonable.

1 1 1 1 1 1 1 1 — 8
Scipio accepted *the price* at once *and* departed happy.

11 1 1 — 4
Flavius sat *in the main room* laughing,

1 1 1 1 — 4
because he had received *so much_money*.

1 1 1 1 1 1 1 — 7
After a few *days* however *Flavius* understood *the truth*:

1 1 1 1 1 1 11 — 8
that shop, which he had *sold* to *the senator*, *had* much *gold hidden*.

1 1 1 1 1 1 1 1 — 8
This *gold* had *lain* for many *years* in the earth *under_the shop*.

1 1 1 1 — 4
Scipio alone had *known* about_*the gold*.

Total mark: 150/3 = [50]

4

1 1 1 1 1 1 1 1 1 1 — 10
Lucius and Sextus were friends. *Lucius* wanted to see *Sextus*.

1 11 1 1 1 — 6
And so *Lucius* sent a slave to_*Sextus*.

11 1 1 1 1 1 1 1 1 1 — 11
The *slave* said, ‘My master is *anxious*. He wants to give you *something*.

1 1 11 1 — 5
You must go at once *to the forum*.’

1 1 1 1 1 1 — 6
And so Lucius hurried *to the forum*, *and* now was looking for *his friend*.

1 1 1 1 1 1 — 6
At last he caught sight of him, *hiding his face*.

1 1 1 1 4
'Why are you *hiding your face*?' *Lucius* asked.

1 1 11 1 1 1 7
'Because three men are seeking me.

1 1 1 1 1 1 1 1 1 1 1 11
They *want* to kill me,' replied *the friend.* 'What have you done?'

1 1 1 1 1 1 11 1 9
'I entered a shop, *because* I *want*ed to *buy* a new *toga*.

1 1 1 1 1 1 6
Suddenly *three men burst in*, holding *swords*.

1 1 1 1 11 1 1 8
They *order*ed the *shopkeeper* to hand over all his money.

1 1 1 1 1 1 1 7
Then they shouted: "Now *give* us *the statue made of gold*."

1 1 1 1 1 11 1 1 9
The shopkeeper, who did not want to *obey*, ran *to*_the door of *the shop*,

1 1 11 1 1 6
but the men cruelly killed him. *Then* they were *looking for the statue*.

1 1 1 1 1 11 1 1 9
When *the men threw* me *to*_the ground, I was terrified.

1 1 1 1 1 11 7
Then I *caught sight of the statue*; I *seized* it *and* fled.

1 1 1 1 1 1 1 7
The men saw me *and attack*ed, *but* they didn't catch *me*.

1 1 1 1 1 1 6
Now they are *seeking* me. *Here's the statue*. I *don't want* to *keep* it.'

1 1 1 1 1 1 1 1 1 1 10
Lucius, who had never *seen* a more beautiful *statue*, was very happy.

Total mark: 150/3 = [50]

5a

1 1 1 1 1 1 1 7
Near the middle of the city was *the temple* of *Jupiter.*

1 1 1 1 1 1 1 1 8
This *temple was* very *ancient and* very beautiful.

11 1 1 1 1 1 1 11 1 1 12
Many people used to come to_*the city* from other *parts* of Italy,

1 1 1 1 1 1 6
because they wanted to see *the temple.*

1 1 1 1 1 1 1 1 8
The priest, who worked in_*the temple*, *was* an old man.

1 11 1 11 1 1 8
This man often led *visitor*s into_*the temple*

1 1 1 1 1 1 6
*and show*ed a huge *statue* of the god,

1 1 1 1 4
which stood in_*the middle of the temple.*

1 1 1 1 4
The statue was made of gold and *ivory.*

1 1 1 1 1 1 1 1 1 1 10
Everyone, when they looked at *the statue*, praised its *beauty and artistry.*

11 1 1 1 1 1 1 1 1 1 1 1 12
One *man* however liked *the gold*, not *the artistry*; this_*man was a thief.*

1 1 1 1 1 1 1 7
As soon as he saw *the statue*, he *decide*d to *steal* it.

1 1 1 1 1 1 1 1 1 9
He had three friends, who were also *thieves.*

1 1 1 1 1 1 1 1 1 9
'*Tomorrow*,' said the first *thief*, '*come* with me to_*the temple of Jupiter.*

1 1 1 1 1 1 11 1 1 1 11
We ought to *have a cart*; we can put *the statue* of *the god* into_*the cart*.'

1 1 1 1 1 1 1 1 8
On the next day four *men* hurried through the *silent* streets of *the city*.

1 1 1 1 1 1 1 1 1 9
It *was the middle of the night*. *No one saw* them entering *the temple*.

1 1 1 1 1 5
The thieves were very happy,

1 1 1 1 1 1 1 7
when, holding *torch*es, they approached *the statue*.

Total mark: 150/3 = [50]

5b

1 1 1 1 1 1 1 1 1 1 10
Once *a thief* with three friends had *decided* to *steal a statue* of a god.

1 1 1 1 1 5
They were now standing in_*the temple* near_*the statue*.

1 1 1 1 11 11 1 1 10
'*How* can we *move the statue*?' asked one of the friends.

1 1 11 1 1 1 1 1 1 10
'*The statue* is huge.' 'It is *certainly* difficult,' replied *the thief*.

1 1 1 1 1 1 1 1 1 1 1 11
'But we *can break off the arms* and head *and the legs*. I have *hammer*s.'

1 1 1 1 1 5
The thief handed *the hammers* to *his friends*.

1 1 1 1 1 1 1 1 1 1 10
When *one_friend struck the statue*, there was a very huge *clang*.

1 1 1 1 1 1 1 11 1 11 1 13
The men were terrified. 'We *can*'t do that,' said *the thief*.

1 1 1 1 1 1 6
'It is *dangerous*. We must *push the statue*.'

1 1 1 1 1 11 1 8
Although *the thieves pushed the statue* with all *their strength*,

1 1 1 1 1 1 1 1 1 1 10
they *could* not *move* it. Suddenly they heard a *terrible* voice:

1 1 1 1 4
'What are you doing, *wicked* men?

1 1 1 1 1 5
Why do you wish to *destroy* my_*statue*?

1 1 1 1 1 1 6
I am now preparing death for you.'

1 11 1 1 5
The thieves fled from_*the temple*, *terrified*.

1 1 1 1 1 5
As soon as *the thieves* departed, *the priest*,

1 1 1 1 1 1 1 7
who had been standing in another *part* of *the temple*,

1 1 1 3
approached *the statue*.

1 1 1 1 1 1 1 11 1 10
'I am a *faithful* servant to you, master,' said *the priest*.

1 1 1 1 1 1 1 7
'*Although* I *am* an old man, my *voice* is *youthful*.'

Total mark: 150/3 = [50]

6

1 11 11 1 1 — 7

Ambiorix had two daughters, *Julia* and *Cornelia*.

1 1 1 1 1 1 1 1 — 8

Ambiorix wanted to choose husbands for the girls.

1 1 1 1 1 1 — 6

The girls however did not want to *have husband*s,

1 1 1 11 — 5

because they feared men.

1 1 1 1 1 — 5

Although he understood *his daughters' fear*,

1 1 1 1 1 — 5

Ambiorix invited his friends to dinner.

1 1 1 11 11 — 7

After they had eaten food, *Ambiorix* said,

1 1 1 1 11 1 1 11 — 10

'*Friend*s, I am looking for *husband*s for my *daughter*s. You *have* sons.

1 1 1 1 1 1 1 11 1 1 1 — 12

Whoever promises me the greatest *dowry* can *choose* a wife.'

1 11 1 1 1 1 1 — 8

At first the friends said nothing; then one *said*,

1 1 1 1 1 1 1 1 1 — 9

'But a *Roman_man* does not give *a dowry* to the father of/for *a girl*;

1 1 1 1 — 4

the father of *the girl gives_a_dowry* to *the husband*.'

1 1 1 1 1 — 5

'It is_*true*,' replied *Ambiorix*. '*But* I am *German*;

1 1 1 1 1 1 1 1 1 — 9

In_*Germany men buy wives*. *My_daughters* are very beautiful;

1 1 1 1 1 1 1 1 1 9
And so it is_*reasonable* to *sell* them. Who *wishes* to *promise* me *gold*?'

1 1 1 1 1 1 1 1 1 9
At last another_*friend said*, 'I do_*not_have a son*, *but my_wife* is now *dead*.

1 11 1 1 1 6
I am *looking* for a new *wife*. *Julia pleases* me.

1 1 1 1 11 1 1 1 9
I am *ready* to *give* you a huge *dowry*. Does it *please* you?'

1 1 1 1 4
'*It pleases*_me,' *replied Ambiorix*, '*but* what about_*Cornelia*?

1 1 1 1 1 5
Surely she also is *beautiful*?'

1 1 1 1 1 1 1 1 8
Soon *another friend put forward his son*. Happy, *Ambiorix agreed*.

Total mark: 150/3 = [50]

7

1 11 1 11 1 1 1 1 11 1 1 14
Appius and Rufina lived in a large house, but they had few slaves.

1 1 1 1 1 11 11 1 1 11
Often it was_*necessary* for *Rufina* to prepare dinner *and* go to the shops,

1 11 1 1 1 1 1 8
because all *the slaves* were doing other things.

1 11 111 1 7
At last *Rufina*, angry, said to her husband:

1 11 1 11 1 7
why don't you buy another *slave*?

11 11 11 1 11 1 1 1 1 1 14
I want to visit friends, not work in_*the house*. I am not a slavegirl.'

1 1 1 1 1 11 1 — 8

Appius, although he didn't want to *spend* money, *agreed*,

1 1 1 1 1 — 5

because he loved his wife.

1 1 1 11 1 1 1 1 1 — 10

And so, when *a slave-dealer* came to the city, *Appius* hurried *to*_him.

1 1 11 1 1 1 1 — 8

The slave-dealer had many *slaves* and *many slavegirls.*

1 1 — 2

*Appius inspect*ed *them all.*

1 1 11 1 — 5

Although Rufina had *want*ed to *buy* a strong *slave*,

1 1 1 1 1 1 — 6

Appius caught sight of a very beautiful *slavegirl.*

1 1 1 11 1 1 — 7

'I *want* to *buy* this girl,' he *said* to *the slave-dealer.*

1 1 11 1 1 1 11 11 — 11

The slave-dealer was happy, because he received much money.

1 1 1 1 — 4

Appius also was very *happy*,

1 1 1 1 1 1 1 — 7

because he had never seen a more *beautiful girl.*

1 1 1 1 — 4

Rufina however was not *happy*,

1 1 1 1 1 1 — 6

because she did not *dare* to leave *the house*:

1 1 1 1 1 1 — 6

for she did *not wish* to *leave her husband* in_*the house* with_*the slavegirl.*

Total mark: 150/3 = [50]

8a

1 11 1 1 1 6
Domitius was a *messenger*. *Domitius* always worked *hard*.

1 1 1 1 1 1 1 1 1 1 1 1 12
He made *long journey*s, carrying letters, which *the emperor* had written.

1 1 1 1 4
By day he *rode*, *by night* he slept in_*roadside inns*;

1 1 1 1 1 1 1 7
in this way the *letters always* quickly reached the men,

11 1 1 1 5
who were expecting them.

1 1 1 1 4
Once he was *making* a very *long_journey*,

1 1 1 1 1 1 1 1 8
for *the emperor* had sent him with_*letters* to_*the chieftains* of *the Gauls*.

1 1 11 1 1 1 7
A large part of *the journey lay* through_*woods*.

1 1 11 1 1 1 1 1 11 1 12
No one else was on the road. Suddenly *Domitius* heard *shout*s.

1 1 1 1 1 1 1 1 8
The voice of a man was shouting: '*Help* me! *Help me!*'

1 1 1 1 1 11 1 8
Domitius at once *jumped down* from_*his horse* and ran through_*the trees*.

1 1 1 1 1 1 1 7
Soon he caught sight of a young man, *tied* to_*a tree*.

1 1 1 1 1 1 1 7
The young man was terrified *and weak*, *for* he had been *there* a long time.

1 11 1 11 1 11 1 11 12
Domitius quickly freed him *and* gave him water and food.

1 1 1 1 1 1 1 7
The young man, as soon as he *recovered his strength*, related *his story*.

1 1 11 1 1 1 7
'When,' *the young man* said, 'I was *riding* through these *woods*,

1 1 1 3
suddenly four_*robbers attacked* me.

1 1 1 1 1 1 6
After they overpowered me *and tied me* to_*the tree*,

1 1 11 1 1 6
they *stole my horse and* all my money.

1 1 1 1 1 1 1 7
I am *lucky* because they did not kill me.

1 1 1 1 1 1 1 7
I am even *luck*ier, because you have now *freed* me.

Total mark: 150/3 = [50]

8b

1 1 1 1 1 1 6
Domitius was making a journey through_*the woods*.

1 1 1 1 4
Domitius, when he *found* a young man,

1 1 1 1 1 1 1 1 8
whom *robbers* had *tied* to_*a tree*, freed him.

1 1 1 1 1 1 1 1 1 1 10
After *Domitius* gave *the young man* food and water,

1 1 1 1 1 1 1 1 11 1 1 12
they returned to the road. However, they could not see *Domitius*' *horse*.

1 11 1 1 5
Domitius was angry,

1 1 1 1 1 1 1 7
because *the horse* was carrying the *emperor*'s letters.

1 1 1 1 1 1 1 1 1 1 10
It was also difficult for *the young man* to walk, because he was *weak*.

1 1 11 1 1 1 1 8
The young man and *Domitius* sat near_*the road*, looking for *a plan*.

1 1 1 1 1 11 1 8
'What ought we to do?' asked *Domitius*.

1 1 1 1 1 1 6
'We can't walk through *such great_woods*.'

1 1 1 1 1 1 6
'When I was *travelling* yesterday,' replied *the young man*,

1 1 1 1 1 1 6
'I came to_*a village*. That_*village* is nearby.

1 1 1 1 4
Perhaps somebody can help us.'

1 11 1 1 1 1 1 8
And so the two men *walk*ed for three *hours*.

1 1 1 1 1 1 11 8
When they approached *the village, the young man* suddenly said:

1 1 1 1 1 1 1 1 1 1 1 11
'I *see* the man, who *tied* me to_*the tree*, entering a house.'

1 1 1 1 1 1 6
Domitius at once dragged *the young man* into_*the woods*.

1 1 1 1 1 5
There they stayed. As soon as it was *night*,

1 1 1 1 1 5
they *burst into_the house and* overpowered *the robber*.

1 1 1 1 1 1 1 7
Then they *got back* everything which *the robbers* had *stolen*.

Total mark: 150/3 = [50]

Section 3: Tests for OCR Foundation Tier

These tests are in three parts. The first and third parts are for comprehension, and the marks are shown for each sub-question. The second part of each test, for translation, is marked differently from the translations in the preceding sections. The passage for translation is divided into five sections, as equal in length as the sentence structure permits. Each of these sections is then marked out of 4, according to the proportion of sense. The following mark descriptors are used:

[4] Perfectly accurate
[3] Overall sense correct; minor error(s) (e.g. tense, number)
[2] Part correct, overall sense lacking / unclear
[1] Not coherent; isolated knowledge of vocabulary only
[0] Totally incorrect or omitted.

This is a very crude scheme but is quick and easy to apply, once a little practice has been gained. Its main drawback is that, especially in longer sections, a wide range of performance can end up with the same mark. Less obvious is the fact that it is impossible to score between 75% and 100% on any one section. In other marking schemes for translation (as used by WJEC), most candidates will fall between these two points on the scale; this means that, in this scheme, the majority of candidates will either perch on the top rung at 100% or (more likely), as a result of one or several errors, be shunted down to 75%; differentiation will inevitably suffer. It should also be noted that, if a candidate makes five major errors (e.g. gets five cases wrong), and these are all in different sections, s/he will score only 50% for the whole translation, even if s/he translates 40 out of 45 words correctly. It is also the case that, whereas isolated vocabulary knowledge allows a candidate to score 1 mark for a section, a similar or even greater knowledge of syntax or accidence without the vocabulary will probably gain no credit at all.

Because of this harshness of the scheme, care must be taken when applying it not to demand too much precision in translations: a near miss in the meaning of a Latin word, or a slight inaccuracy in rendering a particular construction (such as confusing a purpose with a result clause) may have to be allowed. In live examinations examiners will have a list of such minor inaccuracies which they should ignore.

1

Section A

1 the daughter (1) of Clemens (1) [2]
2 the son of Clemens [1]
3 B [1]
4 come (1) with him / me (1) [2]
5 (i) go to the baths [1]
(ii) he was a young man (1) not a boy (1) [2]
6 he had never entered (1) the baths before (1) [2]
7 if she also (1) could visit (1) the baths (1) /
if she (1) could come / go (1) with them (1) [3]
8 (i) go (1) with her mother (1) [2]
(ii) he could take (1) only (1) young men (1) (into the baths) [3]
9 to go to the baths [1]
10 (See Introduction for the mark descriptors.)
(i) *servus quoque ibat. thermae maximae erant.*
(ii) *ubi intraverunt, Septimus attonitus erat, quod palaestra erat plena hominum currentium clamantiumque.*
(iii) *Clemens filium in apodyterium duxit. vestes servo dederunt, quem iusserunt eas custodire.*
(iv) *omnes partes thermarum visitaverunt.*
(v) *tandem Clemens Septimo dixit, 'nunc exibimus; mater tua nos exspectat.'* [20]

Section B

11 they could (1) see (1) neither clothes (1) nor the slave (1) [4]
12 (i) very (1) angry (1) [2]
(ii) look for new tunics [1]
13 his daughter (1) and wife / her mother (1) [2]
14 in the baths (1) his slave (1) found (1) a gold ring (1) [4]
15 (i) where the slave was [1]
(ii) C [1]
(iii) (even) angrier [1]
16 custody (1) being locked up (1)
servile (1) slave-like (1) (accept alternatives) [4]

Total mark: [60]

2

Section A

1 he was a Titan [1]
2 his wife [1]
3 (i) love (1) fear (1) [2]

(ii) he was fierce [1]
4 she had a child / daughter [1]
5 he had heard an oracle (1)
(saying that) his children (1) would kill him (1) [3]
6 (i) ate (1) the child (1) [2]
(ii) when Rhea gave (1) him (1) Vesta / the child (1) to hold (1) [4]
7 B [1]
8 terrified [1]
9 (i) a few years (1) later (1) [2]
(ii) 5 [1]
10 (See Introduction for the mark descriptors.)
(i) *Rhea, postquam filius alius tandem natus est, cui nomen Iovem dedit, eum servare constituit.*
(ii) *primum matri et patri infantem dedit;*
(iii) *deinde, cum Cronus advenisset filium rogans, ei saxum vestibus involutum dedit*
(iv) *et tam vehementer clamabat, ut Cronus saxum consumeret ignarus.*
(v) *postquam Cronus abiit, Rhea cucurrit ut filium teneret.* [20]

Section B
11 he wanted (1) to punish Cronus (1) [2]
12 (i) very good / excellent (1) wine (1) [2]
(ii) he asked (1) for more (1) [2]
13 (i) C [1]
(ii) everything (1) in his stomach (1) [2]
14 the five children (1) he had eaten (1) [2]
15 the fragments clumped together (1) three women (1)
and two men (1) stood near Jupiter / came to life (1) [4]
16 to kill Cronus / him [1]
17 optimist (1) one who expects good fortune (1)
vine (1) the plant that produces grapes (1) (accept alternatives) [4]
Total mark: [60]

3

Section A
1 in a beautiful house [1]
2 many (1) slaves (1) (and) slave-girls (1) [3]
3 (she was) a girl (1) (and) a slave (1) [2]
4 they did together (1) many things (1) [2]
5 (i) go to school (1) with her brothers (1) [2]
(ii) she was a girl [1]
6 teach her [1]
7 D [1]

8 why / if the slave (1) should (not) teach (1) Phoebe as well (1) [3]

9 Phoebe was intelligent (1)
an educated slave-girl (1) has value (1) <greater> (1) [4]

10 (See Introduction for the mark descriptors.)
(i) *tres annos servus duas puellas plurima docebat.*
(ii) *sed Phoebe, cum etiam nunc in villa laboraret, erat tristis.*
(iii) *olim aberat. pater Helenam iussit eam quaerere.*
(iv) *ubi Helena Phoeben vidit in horto sedentem, eam rogavit cur non laboraret.*
(v) *'non laboro,' illa respondit, 'quod iam legere et scribere possum. laborare non volo.'* [20]

Section B

11 to tell him (1) what Phoebe (1) had said (1) [3]

12 (i) more angry [1]
(ii) he didn't want (to have) (1) lazy slaves (1) [2]

13 (i) A: because she called him *carissime* (*vel sim.*)
(Accept a different choice if well argued.) [1]
(ii) D [1]

14 give her / Phoebe (1) better work (1) [2]

15 he loved her / they were close / *vel sim.* [1]

16 (i) real poetry aloud [1]
(ii) when he was entertaining / giving dinner (1) to friends (1) [2]

17 father: he was praised by his friends (1)
Phoebe: she was using her education / intelligence / *vel sim.* [2]

18 narrate (1) tell a story (1)
amicable (1) friendly (1) (accept alternatives) [4]

Total mark: [60]

4

Section A

1 (i) the Greeks (1) captured it (1) [2]
(ii) father (1) son (1) [2]
(iii) all (1) not killed by the Greeks / still alive (1) [2]
(iv) D [1]

2 a huge storm (1) drove the ships to Africa (1) [2]

3 (i) Aeneas' ship [1]
(ii) his father (1) and son (1) had not been killed (1) [3]

4 sad (1) because so many had died (*vel sim.*) (1) [2]

5 (i) seek help [1]
(ii) he could see (i) neither a city nor men (1) [2]

6 a very beautiful (1) girl (1) [2]

7 (See Introduction for the mark descriptors.)

(i) *Aeneas puellam rogavit num ab urbe propinqua venisset.*
(ii) *puella, 'ita vero,' respondit. 'Carthago est nova urbs, quam regina Dido aedificat.*
(iii) *Dido cum multis civibus a patria fugit,*
(iv) *quod frater eam necare volebat, ut ipse rex esset. sed quis es tu?'*
(v) *Aeneas dixit se quoque coactum esse patriam relinquere.* [20]

Section B

8 (i) returned (1) to his men (1) [2]
(ii) Dido's city / Carthage [1]
(iii) A [1]
9 (i) when they entered the city [1]
(ii) temples (1) forum (1) houses (1) [3]
10 in the middle [1]
11 (i) Aeneas / a Trojan prince (1) had arrived (1) [2]
(ii) she was very happy [1]
12 (i) the Trojan War (1) the courage of Aeneas (1) [2]
(ii) an excellent (1) dinner (1) [2]
13 medium (1) mid-range (1)
navy (1) sea-borne forces (1) (accept alternatives) [4]

Total mark: [60]

5

Section A

1 (he was) the priest (1) of (the goddess) Isis (1) [2]
2 (i) very / many citizens worshipped her [1]
(ii) she promised (1) (another) life after death (1) [2]
3 B [1]
4 leading a procession (1) through the (middle of the) city (1)
carrying (1) the statue of the goddess (1) [4]
5 watch (1) the procession / statue / goddess (1) [2]
6 in the (middle of the) forum (1) on the ground (1) [2]
7 good fortune (1) (very) much corn (1) [2]
8 she will (always) protect (1) the city (1)
she will give (1) (very) good fortune (1) [4]
9 (See Introduction for the mark descriptors.)
(i) *omnes cives erant laetissimi.*
(ii) *sed erat unus vir, Petrus, qui, cum esset Christianus, alios deos videre nolebat;*
(iii) *Christo solo credebat. Petrus tam iratus erat ut inter principes curreret.*
(iv) *'Isis non est dea,' clamavit.*
(v) *'Christus solus vos servare potest. Christum, non Isidem, colite.'* [20]

Section B

10 go away [1]
11 excellent / the best / very good (goddess) [1]
12 A [1]
13 in the name (1) of Christ (1) I curse you all (1)
Christ will punish you (1) [4]
14 he was captured (1) and imprisoned (1) [2]
15 many citizens (1) were killed (1) [2]
16 he laughed [1]
17 his god / Christ (1) has punished them (1) [2]
18 they would not worship (1) so cruel a god (1) [2]
19 nominate (1) call / name (1)
capture (1) take prisoner (1) (accept alternatives) [4]

Total mark: [60]

Section 4: Tests for OCR Higher Tier

These tests are identical in format to those of the previous section. The marking of them is, therefore, also the same. For convenience, the mark descriptors are repeated here:

[4] Perfectly accurate
[3] Overall sense correct; minor error(s) (e.g. tense, number)
[2] Part correct, overall sense lacking / unclear
[1] Not coherent; isolated knowledge of vocabulary only
[0] Totally incorrect or omitted.

1

Section A

1 brothers [1]

2 (i) he died [1]
(ii) he would be king [1]
(iii) he was the elder [1]

3 he drove out his brother (1) from the city / to be king himself (1) [2]

4 (i) they were killed [1]
(ii) she was forced (1) to be a Vestal Virgin (1) [2]
(iii) so she would not have a son [1]

5 (i) death [1]
(ii) if she slept (1) with a man (1) [2]

6 (i) remove rivals [1]
(ii) she gave birth (1) to two (1) sons (1) [3]

7 who was (1) the father (1) of the (two) boys (1) [3]

8 (See Introduction for the mark descriptors.)
(i) *rex iratus pueros militibus tradidit, ut eos in flumine necarent.*
(ii) *milites tamen pueros in canistrum posuerunt; hoc magna cum cura in flumen posuerunt,*
(iii) *deos orantes ut pueros servarent. flumen canistrum ad ripam tulit.*
(iv) *ibi lupa pueros lacrimantes audivit. lupa pueris lac dedit. ita Romulus Remusque servati sunt.*
(v) *tandem pastor eos inventos ad uxorem portavit; quae eos multos annos educabat.* [20]

Section B

9 to seize their booty [1]

10 they divided among them (1) all the booty (1) [2]

11 (i) when they found this out [1]
(ii) (began to) come together [1]

12 (i) even more were being attacked / they were losing much money [1]
(ii) they made an ambush (1) against the young men (1) [2]

13 (i) resisted bravely [1]
(ii) captured (1) dragged / taken to Amulius (1) [2]

14 leading (1) a crowd of young men (1) against Numitor's land (1) [3]

15 he trusted neither / not the bandits (1) nor / not Remus (1)
(Allow 1 for 'to be punished'.) [2]

16 plural (1) more than one (1)
conduct (1) lead (1) (accept alternatives) [4]

Total mark: [60]

2

Section A

1 captured by bandits (1) taken to Numitor (1) [2]

2 punishing Remus [1]

3 he saw Remus (1) he found out (1) he had a brother (1) [3]
4 who is your father / who was his father [1]
5 a she-wolf saved them (1) from the river (1)
a shepherd and his wife (1) brought them up (1) [4]
6 (i) his two grandsons [1]
(ii) they should have been killed [1]
(iii) he thought Romulus and Remus could be his grandsons [1]
7 when he found out (1) what Amulius had done (1) [2]
8 (i) Remus (1) Romulus (1) the rest of the young men (1) [3]
(ii) Amulius was killed [1]
9 (See Introduction for the mark descriptors.)
(i) *cives, ubi Romulus Remusque Numitorem regem salutaverunt, plauserunt.*
(ii) *cum Numitor iam esset rex Albae Longae, Romulus et Remus sibi novam urbem aedificare volebant,*
(iii) *prope locum in quo inventi erant. sed difficile erat fratribus constituere*
(iv) *uter dux esse deberet. deos igitur oraverunt ut sibi signum darent.*
(v) *signo a deis ad Romulum misso, Romulus a civibus rex salutatus est.* [20]

Section B
10 his brother / Romulus (1) not he himself (1)
had been chosen king (1) by the citizens (1) [4]
11 accept this [1]
12 Romulus and his friends (1) were building them (1)
Remus laughed at them (1) (any two) [2]
13 (i) very small [1]
(ii) he could jump over them (1) easily (1) [2]
14 (i) he saw Remus (1) jumping over the walls (1) [2]
(ii) he killed Remus [1]
15 because they were faithful (1) to Romulus (1) [2]
16 more powerful [1]
17 civic (1) relating to the city (1)
solitary (1) on ones own (1) (accept alternatives) [4]
Total mark: [60]

3

Section A
1 king (1) of the new city (1) [2]
2 (i) many (1) friends (1) [2]
(ii) look for / find (1) more citizens (1) [2]
3 many men (1) fled to the refuge (1) from neighbouring cities (1) [3]
4 escaped slaves (1)
(wicked) men who had stolen money (1) (or) killed men (1) [3]

5 no women [1]
6 how to persuade (1) women (1) to come to the city (1) [3]
7 to invite people to Rome / a show [1]
8 (i) go to Rome [1]
(ii) to see the show (1) (and) the new city (1) [2]
9 (See Introduction for the mark descriptors.)
(i) *hospites in villas Romanorum laete accepti sunt.*
(ii) *novo foro et omnibus templis conspectis, attoniti erant cum cognovissent urbem tam celeriter aedificatam esse.*
(iii) *ubi omnes parati erant spectaculum spectare, Romulus signum dedit. subito iuvenes Romani ad hospites cucurrerunt.*
(iv) *omnes virgines, quae cum parentibus Romam venerant, raptas ad villas suas portaverunt.*
(v) *parentes earum, qui nulla arma secum habebant, discesserunt tristissimi.* [20]

Section B
10 (i) the Romans had seized / captured them [1]
(ii) they persuaded their leaders (1) to attack Rome (1) [2]
11 the Romans defeated them (1) easily (1) [2]
12 (i) happier [1]
(ii) they had been captured / treated cruelly / badly [1]
(iii) they had been given love (1) gifts (1) beautiful houses (1) [3]
13 (i) bigger [1]
(ii) shouted for peace [1]
14 turn against us / them (1) anger and swords (1) [2]
15 they would rather die (1) than live without menfolk (1) [2]
16 urban (1) belonging to the city (1)
novelty (1) something new (1) (accept alternatives) [4]
Total mark: [60]

4

Section A
1 king of Clusium [1]
2 (i) the Etruscans (1) had founded it (1) many years before (1) [3]
(ii) it had great power [1]
3 (i) the king, Tarquinius (1) was expelled (1) [2]
(ii) to seek (1) his help (1) [2]
(iii) he was Etruscan [1]
4 (i) fight together [1]
(ii) they are both Etruscan [1]
5 he feared (1) the (growing) power of Rome (1) [2]
6 (i) led a large army (1) into Roman territory (1) [2]
(ii) flee into the city [1]

7 (i) enter the city [1]
(ii) part was defended by walls (1) part by the river (1) [2]

8 (See Introduction for the mark descriptors.)
(i) *sed pons erat, qui hostibus viam ad mediam urbem dare poterat.*
(ii) *pauci milites Romani hunc pontem custodiebant sed, hostibus conspectis, fugere volebant.*
(iii) *Horatius tamen eis persuasit ut manerent.*
(iv) *'si vultis,' inquit, 'hostibus urbem tradere, fugite; si tamen libertatem cupitis, mecum manete pontemque delete.'*
(v) *Romani, his verbis victi, pontem delere coeperunt. interea Horatius in ponte solus stabat, hostes exspectans.* [20]

Section B

9 (i) jumped into the river [1]
(ii) when the bridge was destroyed [1]

10 because he couldn't enter [1]

11 (i) kill Porsenna [1]
(ii) after many days [1]

12 he didn't know (1) the king (1)
he killed his scribe (1) not the king (1) [4]

13 ordered soldiers (1) to kill the yound man (1)
having captured him (1) [3]

14 many other young men (1) want to kill him (1) [2]

15 (i) leave Rome / lead his troops from Rome [1]
(ii) they had been saved / were safe [1]

16 regal (1) like a king (1)
intellectual (1) a clever person (1) (accept alternatives) [4]

Total mark: [60]

5

Section A

1 king of Athens [1]

2 (i) a wife [1]
(ii) sons (1) daughters (1) [2]

3 (i) to have a son [1]
(ii) to seek the advice (1) of friends (1) [2]

4 he was Aegeus' friend (1) he was a king (1)
he had a (very) beautiful daughter (1) [3]

5 he fell in love with her / loved her at once (1) [1]

6 (i) one night [1]
(ii) sad [1]
(iii) because he wanted to stay (*vel sim.*) [1]
(iv) he loved her [1]

7 (i) return home / to Athens [1]

(ii) his wife (1) was waiting for / expecting him (1) [2]

8 because Aegeus was going / had decided to go [1]

9 give him a son [1]

10 (See Introduction for the mark descriptors.)

(i) *Aethra filium peperit. puero nomen Theseum dedit.*

(ii) *paucis annis Theseus sapientior fortiorque erat quam omnes alii pueri.*

(iii) *ubi Theseus iuvenis erat, mater ei, 'in silvam festina,' inquit; 'ibi magnum saxum videbis.*

(iv) *sub saxo gladium invenies, quem pater tuus celavit. fer mihi illum gladium.'*

(v) *Theseus in silvam cucurrit, ut saxum peteret; quo conspecto mox gladium invenit.* [20]

Section B

11 (i) when he found the sword [1]

(ii) the sword was rusty [1]

(iii) he realised his father (1) had worn / carried the sword (1) [2]

(iv) took it (1) to his mother (1) [2]

12 praised her son (1) cried (1) [2]

13 it was his father's (1) he put it under the rock (1) [2]

14 give me / him a son (1) send him to me / him (1) with the sword (1) [3]

15 go to Athens [1]

16 (i) who his father was [1]

(ii) ask when he got to Athens [1]

17 primary (1) the first stage (1)

porter (1) a person who carries (1) (accept alternatives) [4]

Total mark: [60]

Section 5: Tests for WJEC Level 2 Core

Each of these tests is in three parts. The first and third parts contain a similar range of comprehension questions to the Level 1 Core tests, and should be marked in a similar way. The second section is translation, and should be marked in exactly the same way as that of the Level 1 Additional tests in Section 2. In the examination, the raw total for the translation is normally 140; here it is either 130 or 140, depending on the proportion of glossed or repeated words. A calculator or the scaling chart (Appendix) should be used for scaling the mark down to 40.

1

(a) he was a Titan / among the Titans [1]
(b) the wife of Cronus [1]
(c) (i) love (1) fear (1) [2]
 (ii) he was cruel [1]
(d) (i) *laeta* (1) happy (1) [2]
 (ii) she had a daughter [1]
 (iii) *pulchrae* (1) beautiful (1) [2]
(e) A,D,F [3]
(f) he devised (1) a dreadful (1) plan (1) [3]
(g) (i) handed Vesta (1) to Cronus (1) [2]
 (ii) so that he could hold (1) her (1) [2]
 (iii) he ate (1) Vesta / her (1) [2]
 (iv) trade / tradition / tradesman [1]
(h) (i) B [1]
 (ii) terrified / frightened / scared [1]

Total [25]

2

1 1 1 1 1 1 1 1 1 1 11 1 1 [14]
When after a few years a son was_*born*, *Cron*us ate him too.

1 1 1 1 1 1 1 1 1 1 1 [11]
In this way three other *children*, as soon as they were *born*, perished.

1 1 1 1 1 1 11 1 1 1 1 [12]
Rhea didn't know what she could do; for she wanted *children*,

1 1 1 1 1 1 1 [7]
but didn't want to hand them over to *Cron*us.

1 1 1 1 1 1 1 1 1 1 1 [11]
After *another son was* finally *born*, to whom she gave the name *Jupiter*,

1 1 1 1 1 1 11 [8]
Rhea thought up an excellent plan.

1 1 1 1 1 1 1 1 [8]
First(ly) she *gave the baby* to *her* mother and father;

1 1 1 1 1 1 1 1 [8]
then, when *Cronus* arrived, demanding *his son*,

1 1 1 1 1 [5]
she *hand*ed him *a stone wrapped* in *clothes*.

1 1 1 1 1 1 1 1 [8]
While she was *giv*ing him this, she was shouting *and* crying so loudly,

1 1 1 1 1 [5]
that *Cronus ate the stone without realising*.

1 1 1 1 1 1 [6]
After *Cronus* went away happ(il)y,

1 1 1 1 1 1 1 1 1 [9]
Rhea hurried even more *happy* to *her mother* and *father*,

1 1 1 1 1 1 [6]
who already had hidden *Jupiter* in_*a cave*.

1 1 1 1 [4]
There they looked after him.

1 1 1 1 1 1 1 1 [8]
When *Jupiter* was *grown up*, he decided to *punish Cronus*.

Total mark = [130]; convert to a mark out of [40]. Total : [40]

3

(a) B,C,E [3]

(b) (i) who (1) he / Jupiter was (1) [2]

(ii) never (1) had he seen him (1) before (1) [3]

(c) ask for (1) more (1) [2]
(d) (i) C [1]
(ii) everything (1) contained (1) in his stomach (1) [3]
(e) A,D,E [3]
(f) C [1]
(g) three (1) women (1) (and) two (1) men (1) stood (1) by Jupiter (1) [6]
(h) (i) who (1) are you (1) [2]
(ii) your (1) children (1) [2]

(i) (i) punish him / Cronus [1]
(ii) he had killed (1) them (1) [2]

(j) (i) D [1]
(ii) *patrem* [1]
(k) king (1) of the gods (1) [2]
Total [35]

2

1
(a) B [1]
(b) (i) it was destroyed (1) by the Greeks (1) [2]
(ii) father (1) son (1) [2]
(iii) all (1) not killed (1) by the Greeks (1) [3]
(iv) D [1]
(c) A,D [2]
(d) a huge storm (1) drove the ships (1) to Africa (1) [3]
(e) (i) Aeneas' [1]
(ii) *laetissimus* (1) very happy (1) [2]
(iii) (because) his father (1) and son (1) were alive (1) [3]
(f) sad / upset (1) so many were dead / too few left to found a city (1) [2]
(g) (i) walked to the top of / climbed (1) a hill (1) [2]
(ii) to look round [1]
Total [25]

2
1 1 1 1 1 1 1 1 1 1 1 [11]
Aeneas wanted to look at the land, to which he had come.

1 1 1 1 1 11 [7]
For he wanted to seek help,

1 1 1 11 1 1 1 1 1 1 [11]
But he could see neither a city nor people / men.

1 1 1 1 1 1 1 11 1 1 1 [12]
When he was standing there, a very beautiful girl approached him.

1 1 1 1 1 [5]
Aeneas, after he greeted *the girl*,

1 1 1 1 1 1 1 [7]
asked her whether she had *come* from *a nearby city / town*.

1 1 1 1 1 1 11 [8]
The girl replied, '*Yes*. The name of *the city* is *Carthage*.

1 1 11 1 1 1 1 1 [9]
Carthage is a new *city*, which *Queen Dido* is building quickly.

1 11 1 1 11 1 [8]
Dido fled from_*her homeland* with many citizens,

1 1 1 1 1 1 1 [7]
because her brother *want*ed to kill her,

1 1 1 1 11 1 1 1 1 1 [11]
so that he himself *could* hold power. *But* who are you?

1 1 11 1 1 1 11 [9]
Aeneas willingly told *the girl* the whole story / thing.

1 1 1 1 1 1 [6]
Then *the girl*, *change*d into *the appearance* of a goddess,

1 11 1 1 11 1 1 1 [10]
suddenly left him: *for the girl* was *Venus*, the mother of *Aeneas*.

1 1 11 1 1 1 1 1 [9]
Aeneas was angry, because *his mother* had *deceived* him so.

Total mark = [130]; convert to a mark out of [40]. Total : [40]

3

(a) D [1]

(b) (i) Aeneas (1) (and) a few (1) friends (1) [3]

(ii) *Didonis* (1) Dido's (1) [2]

(c) (i) as they approached (1) the city (1) [2]

(ii) building (1) temples (1) forum (1) (and) houses (1) [4]

(iii) multitude / multiply etc. [1]

(d) (i) in the middle [1]

(ii) very (1) beautiful (1) [2]

(e) B,C,F [3]
(f) (i) Dido / the queen [1]
(ii) Aeneas (1) told her (1) his name (1) [3]
(g) B [1]
(h) (i) (much about) the Trojan (1) War (1)
(and) the courage (1) of Aeneas (1) [4]
(ii) prepare (1) an excellent (1) dinner /meal (1)
for you / the Trojans (1) [4]
(i) A,D,E [3]
Total [35]

3

1
(a) King of Athens [1]
(b) (i) a wife [1]
(ii) sons (1) daughters (1) [2]
(c) (i) to have (1) a son (1) [2]
(ii) to seek (1) the help (1) of his friends (1) [3]
(d) A,C,F [3]
(e) (i) *diu* (1) (for) a long time (1) [2]
(ii) (he had) a very beautiful (1) daughter (1) [2]
(f) C [1]
(g) he loved / fell in love with (1) her (1) [2]
(h) (i) *unam noctem* (1) one night (1) [2]
(ii) sad [1]
(i) (i) return home / to Athens [1]
(ii) his wife (1) was expecting / waiting for him (1) [2]
Total [25]

2

1 11 11 1 1 1 1 1 1 [11]
Aethra was sad, because *Aegeus* had decided to leave.

1 1 1 1 1 1 1 1 11 1 1 1 [13]
Aegeus, *before* he left *Aethra*, begged her to give him a son;

1 1 1 11 1 1 1 1 1 [10]
then he left. Nine *months* after, *Aethra gave birth to a son*.

1 1 1 1 1 1 1 [7]
She gave the boy the name *Theseus*.

1 1 1 1 1 1 1 [7]
Aethra herself taught *Theseus* so well,

1 1 1 1 11 1 111 1 11 1 1 1 [16]
that soon he was *wise*r and braver than all the other *boy*s.

1 1 1 1 1 [5]
When *Theseus was* a young man,

1 1 11 1 11 1 1 [9]
his mother said to him, 'Hurry into the wood.

1 1 1 1 11 1 1 1 [9]
For in the middle of *the wood* is a large *rock*.

1 11 1 1 1 1 11 1 1 11 [13]
Under_*the rock* lies a sword, which your father hid.

11 1 1 1 [5]
Bring me that *sword*.'

1 11 1 1 1 1 1 1 1 1 [11]
Theseus ran into_*the wood*, to look for *the rock*; *soon* he saw it.

1 1 1 1 1 1 1 1 [8]
At first he could not *move the rock*, although he *push*ed (it).

1 1 1 1 1 1 1 1 [8]
He walked around_*the rock*, looking at it angr(il)y.

1 1 1 1 11 11 [8]
Then he was *able_to_move_it* from only one *direction*.

Total mark = [140]; convert to a mark out of [40]. Total : [40]

3

(a) moved the rock [1]
(b) (i) under the rock [1]
(ii) sought (1) by him (1) [2]
(c) (i) *iratus* (1) angry (1) [2]
(ii) the sword (1) was rusty (1) [2]
(iii) *deinde* [1]
(iv) his father (1) had worn (1) the sword (1) [3]
(v) took it (1) happily (1) to his mother (1) [3]
(d) B,C,F [3]
(e) (i) paternal / paternity etc. [1]
(ii) D [1]
(iii) hid (1) the sword (1) under the rock (1) [3]

(f) (i) Aegeus [1]
(ii) Aegeus [1]
(iii) Aethra [1]

(g) (i) Aethra to give him (1) a son (1) [2]
(ii) afterwards (1) send (1) him (1) with the sword (1) to me / him (1) [5]

(h) go / travel / make a journey (1) to Athens (1) [2]

Total [35]

4

1

(a) son (1) of Aethra (1) [2]

(b) (i) the sword (1) of his father (1) [2]
(ii) *iuvenis* (1) a young man (1) [2]

(c) ordered him (1) to go (1) to Athens (1) [3]

(d) C [1]

(e) (i) long (1) very dangerous (1) [2]
(ii) many robbers (1) attack (1) travellers (1) [3]

(f) ship [1]

(g) A,D,E [3]

(h) (i) go to the palace (1) show (1) that / the sword (1) to the king (1) [4]
(ii) the king (1) will answer his questions (*vel.sim.*) (1) [2]

Total [25]

2

1 1 1 1 1 1 1 1 1 1 [10]
Although *Aethra* had ordered him to go to_*Athens* in a ship,

1 1 1 1 1 1 1 [7]
Theseus did not want to cross the sea.

1 1 11 1 1 1 1 [8]
Carrying food and the sword, therefore,

1 1 1 1 1 1 [6]
he left his mother, *stricken* with *fear*.

1 1 1 1 [4]
He was not afraid of *the robbers*,

1 1 1 1 1 1 [6]
about whom *his mother* had warned him.

1 1 1 1 1 1 1 1 [8]
For he was a very brave young man.

11 11 1 1 11 1 1 [10]
The first part of the journey lay through a wood.

1 1 1 1 1 1 1 1 1 1 [10]
When he approached the middle of the *wood*, he heard a shout.

1 1 1 1 1 11 [7]
Soon he caught sight of a huge man,

1 1 1 11 1 1 1 [8]
who was pulling the top of *a tree* to the ground.

1 1 1 1 1 1 1 11 11 1 [12]
He, as soon as he saw *Theseus*, shouted: 'I am *Sinis*. Help me.'

1 1 1 1 1 1 1 1 [8]
'What do you want to do?' asked *Theseus*.

1 1 1 1 1 1 1 [7]
'I *want* to *tie* this *tree* to_*the ground*,' *Sinis* replied.

1 1 1 1 1 1 1 [7]
Although he did not know why *Sinis* wanted *to do* this,

1 1 1 1 1 1 [6]
Theseus willingly *help*ed him. *Soon* they *tied the top of the tree*.

1 1 1 1 1 1 1 1 [8]
When *Theseus* began to depart, the *man shout*ed:

11 1 1 1 1 1 1 [8]
'Wait! I want to *tie* another *tree*.'

Total mark = [140]; convert to a mark out of [40]. Total : [40]

3
(a) B [1]
(b) tied to the ground (1) the head (1) of another tree (1) [3]
(c) (i) attacked (1) Theseus (1) [2]
(ii) as soon as (1) they finished (1) [2]
(d) A,D,E [3]
(e) (i) what (1) Sinis wanted (1) to do (1) [3]
(ii) *iratus* (1) angry (1) [2]
(iii) what Sinis (1) had wanted (1) to do (1) [3]
(f) (i) tied (1) Sinis' arms (1) to two (1) trees (1) [4]

(ii) cut the ropes (1) with his sword (1) [2]
(iii) holding the trees (1) to the ground (1) [2]
(iv) terrain / territory etc. [1]
(g) he was torn (1) in two (1) [2]
(h) (i) *gaudens* (1) glad / rejoicing (1) [2]
(ii) he had defeated (1) a very cruel (1) robber (1) [3]
Total [35]

5

1
(a) B [1]
(b) a few (1) hours (1) [2]
(c) (i) *altum* [1]
(ii) it had rained (1) for a long time (1) [2]
(d) cross (1) the river (1) [2]
(e) he stood (there) (1) wondering (1) what (1) he ought (1) to do (1) [5]
(f) a young man [1]
(g) (i) come / go (1) with me / him (1) [2]
(ii) local / location / locus / etc. [1]
(iii) A,D,F [3]
(h) (i) *laetior* (1) happier (1) [2]
(ii) he didn't have to stay (1) near the river (1) [2]
(i) the young man [1]
Total [25]

2
1 1 1 1 1 1 1 1 1 1 1 [11]
'Help me!' the young man shouted. 'I can't *swim*.'

1 11 1 1 1 1 1 [8]
Theseus, who *could swim*, at once *leapt down* into the river.

1 1 1 1 1 1 1 11 1 [10]
Soon he held *the young man*; then he dragged him to_*the bank*.

1 11 1 1 1 1 1 1 1 1 [11]
The young man was so *grateful*, that he decided to tell *Theseus*

1 1 11 1 1 11 [8]
what sort of man his master was.

11 1 1 1 11 1 1 1 1 1 1 1 [14]
'My *master*,' he said, 'is *Procrustes*. *Procrustes* is a very cruel man.

1 1 1 1 1 1 1 1 1 1 1 11 11 [15]
He sent me to_*the river*, to look for *a traveller* and *invite* him *to* our house.

1 1 1 1 1 1 1 1 1 1 1 [11]
However, he always kills *the guests*. It is *necessary* for you to kill him.'

1 1 1 1 1 [5]
After they came to_*the house* of *Procrustes*,

1 1 1 1 1 1 1 [7]
Procrustes willingly prepared dinner for *Theseus*;

1 1 1 1 1 [5]
then he led him to_*a bedroom*.

1 1 1 1 1 11 1 [8]
There he persuaded *Theseus* to lie on_*the bed*.

1 1 111 1 1 1 11 [10]
'You are longer than *the bed*,' *Procrustes* said.

1 1 1 11 11 [7]
'It is *necessary* for me to *cut off* your feet.'

Total mark = [130]; convert to a mark out of [40]. Total : [40]

3

(a) *crudelissimus* (1) very (1) cruel (1) [3]
(b) kill (1) Theseus (1) [2]
(c) B,C,F [3]
(d) (i) much (1) stronger (1) than Procrustes (1) [3]
 (ii) he seized (1) the axe (1) [2]
 (iii) short, because of *facile* [1]
(e) his feet (1) were cut off (1) (*vel sim.*) on the bed (1) [3]
(f) (i) he had brought (1) Theseus (1) to the house (1) [3]
 (ii) *laetissimus* (1) very (1) happy (1) [3]
 (iii) Theseus had killed (1) his master (1)
 his master's (1) death (1) had freed him (1) [5]
(g) (i) rejoicing (1) burying (1) his (dead) master (1) [3]
 (ii) B [1]
(h) (i) two (1) days (1) [2]
 (ii) urban / suburban / urbane / etc. [1]

Total [35]

6

1

(a) brave (1) young man (1) [2]
(b) defeated (1) two brigands (1) [2]
(c) he wanted (1) to find out / know (1) who was (1) his father (1) [4]
(d) (i) looked for (1) the palace (1) [2]
(ii) the middle [1]
(iii) media / median / mediate / medium / etc. [1]
(e) A,D [2]
(f) (i) near (1) the door (1) [2]
(ii) to look for (1) the king (1) [2]
(g) the queen (1) not the king / came to him (1) [2]
(h) (i) D [1]
(ii) looked (1) closely (1) at Theseus (1) and his sword (1) [4]
Total [25]

2

1 1 1 1 1 1 11 1 [9]
Medea, after she looked at *Theseus*, at last said to him:

11 1 1 1 1 1 1 1 1 1 1 1 1 1 [15]
'King *Aegeus* is away. If you want to see him, come to dinner.

1 1 1 [3]
Now go away.'

1 1 1 1 1 1 1 1 1 1 1 1 1 [13]
Theseus therefore walked through the city, to look at the beautiful temples.

1 11 1 1 1 1 1 1 1 1 1 [12]
After three hours he returned to_*the palace*, wearing his sword.

1 1 1 1 1 1 1 1 1 1 1 [12]
The queen herself opened the door and received him into_*the palace*.

1 1 1 1 1 1 11 [8]
Medea however had conceived a dreadful plan,

1 1 1 1 1 1 1 1 1 11 [11]
because, as soon as she saw *the sword*, she realised who *Theseus* was.

1 1 1 1 1 1 1 1 1 1 1 1 [12]
For her husband had left that *sword*, when he was *visiting* a friend.

1 1 1 11 1 1 1 [8]
'Do you *want* to *drink* some wine?' *the queen* asked.
1 1 1 1 1 [5]
At once she handed *a cup of wine* to *Theseus.*

1 1 1 1 1 1 1 1 1 1 [9]
But *before Theseus* could *drink the wine*, *the king* suddenly entered.

1 1 1 1 1 [5]
He too, *as soon as* he saw *the sword*, *realised who Theseus was.*

1 1 1 1 1 1 1 1 [8]
Then *the king noticed the cup of wine*, which *Theseus* was holding.

Total mark = [130]; convert to a mark out of [40]. Total : [40]

3

(a) (i) *perterritus* (1) terrified (1) [2]
(ii) when he saw the cup of wine [1]
(b) his wife (1) often (1) had put poison (1) in it (1) [4]
(c) what (1) his wife / she was doing (1)
why (1) she wanted (1) to kill (1) the young man (1) [6]
(d) A,D,E [3]
(e) (i) D [1]
(ii) he ran (1) to Theseus (1) threw the cup (1) to the ground (1) [4]
(f) the wine contained poison / acid (1) when this touched the floor (1)
it dissolved the stone (1) (accept less precise answers) [3]
(g) *attonitus* [1]
(h) (i) Theseus was / you are (1) his / my son (1) [2]
(ii) seeing him [1]
(i) (i) kill him / Theseus [1]
(ii) go away [1]
(iii) he didn't want (1) to see her (1) again (1) [3]
(j) he knew (1) who his father was (1) [2]

Total [35]

7

1

(a) brothers [1]
(b) (i) he died [1]
(ii) Numitor (1) ought to have been king (1) [2]
(iii) he was the elder [1]
(iv) mortal / mortuary / immortal / etc. [1]
(c) A,D,E [3]
(d) (i) the king / Amulius (1) killed them (1) [2]
(ii) the daughter of Numitor [1]

(iii) she was forced (1) to be (1) a Vestal Virgin (1) [3]

(e) (i) death [1]

(ii) for sleeping (1) with a man (1) [2]

(f) (i) D [1]

(ii) to remove rivals [1]

(iii) she gave birth to (1) two (1) sons (1) [3]

(iv) angry (*vel sim.*) [1]

(v) because he now had rivals to the throne (*vel sim.*) [1]

Total [25]

2

1 1 1 1 1 1 11 1 1 1 11 1 [14]
When *Amulius* asked *Rhea Silvia* who was the father of the two sons,

11 1 1 1 1 11 1 1 1 11 1 [14]
she replied, '*Mars.*' The angry king, after he threw her in_*prison*,

1 1 1 1 1 1 1 11 1 1 1 1 [13]
handed the boys to soldiers, to kill them in the river.

1 1 1 1 1 11 1 1 11 [11]
The soldiers however, because they didn't want to do this,

1 1 1 1 [4]
placed *the boys* in_*a basket*;

1 1 1 11 1 1 [7]
they *plac*ed this with great care in_*the river*,

1 1 1 1 1 1 1 1 [8]
begging the gods to save *the boy*s.

1 11 1 1 1 1 1 1 [9]
After three hours *the river* bore *the basket* to_*the bank*.

1 1 1 1 1 1 1 1 1 [9]
There *a she-wolf*, which had come from the mountains to_*the river*,

1 1 11 1 1 1 1 1 [9]
to *drink* water, heard *the boys* crying.

1 1 1 1 1 [5]
The wolf provided *milk* for *the boys*,

1 1 1 1 1 1 [6]
whom she had carried from_*the basket* into a wood.

1 1 1 1 1 [5]
Thus *Romulus* and *Remus* were looked after / saved.

1 1 1 1 1 11 1 1 [9]
At last *a shepherd* found them and took *them* to his wife;

1 1 1 1 1 1 1 [7]
she *brought* them *up* for many years.

Total mark = [130]; convert to a mark out of [40]. Total : [40]

3

(a) (i) attacked (1) bandits (1) [2]
(ii) to seize (1) their booty (1) [2]
(b) they divided the booty (1) among them (1) [2]
(c) A,D,F,H [4]
(d) (i) *irati* (1) angry (1) [2]
(ii) they had lost so much booty (*vel sim.*) [1]
(iii) they made (1) an ambush (1) against the young men (1) [3]
(e) (i) resisted (1) bravely (1) [2]
(ii) he was captured (1) and dragged (1) to Amulius (1) [3]
(f) (i) leading (1) a band (1) of young men (1)
against Numitor's land (1) [4]
(ii) no / partly (1) it wasn't Numitor's land they were plundering (1) [2]
(g) (i) *iuvenem* (1) young man (1) [2]
(ii) he handed him (1) to Numitor (1) [2]
(iii) he didn't trust (1) the bandits (1) or Remus (1) [3]
(iv) he would be punished [1]

Total [35]

8

1

(a) they were brothers [1]
(b) (i) captured (1) by bandits (1) [2]
(ii) he was being led (1) to Numitor (1) [2]
(c) (i) D [1]
(ii) whether Remus (1) should be punished (1) [2]
(d) he didn't trust them [1]
(e) A,D,E [3]
(f) (i) who is (1) your father (1) [2]

(ii) *plenus spei* (1) full (1) of hope (1) [3]

(g) I don't know [1]

(h) a she-wolf saved them (1) from the river (1)
a shepherd and his wife (1) brought them up (1) [4]

(i) (i) his two grandsons [1]
(ii) killed [1]
(iii) he had found his grandsons [1]

Total [25]

2

1 1 1 1 1 1 1 1 1 1 1 1 1 [13]
When *Remus* learned what *Amulius* had done, he was very angry.

1 1 1 1 1 1 1 1 1 [9]
At once *Remus* with his brother and the rest of the young men

1 1 1 1 1 1 1 1 [8]
attacked *Amulius* and his friends so fiercely,

1 1 1 1 1 1 1 1 1 1 [10]
that in a very short time they killed the king.

1 1 1 1 1 1 1 1 1 1 [10]
Then *Numitor* announced to the assembled citizens everything

11 1 1 [4]
that had happened.

1 1 1 1 1 1 [6]
When *Romulus and Remus*, walking through the crowd,

1 1 1 1 1 1 1 1 [8]
greeted *Numitor* as *king*, *the citizens clap*ped joyfully.

1 1 1 1 1 [5]
Since *Numitor* was *king* of *Alba Longa*,

1 1 1 1 1 1 11 11 [10]
Romulus and Remus wanted to build for themselves a new city,

1 1 1 1 1 1 1 11 [9]
near the river in which *the she-wolf* had found them.

1 1 1 1 1 1 1 1 1 1 [10]
But because *the brother*s were *twins*, it was difficult to decide

1 1 1 1 1 1 1 1 [8]
which one of them ought to be the leader.

1 1 1 1 1 1 11 11 1 1 [12]
They therefore begged the gods to give them a sign.

1 1 11 1 1 11 1 [9]
Although *Remus* saw six *vultures* sent by the *gods*,

1 11 1 [4]
Romulus saw twelve.

1 1 1 1 1 [5]
Romulus was therefore *greeted* by *the citizens* as *king*.

Total mark = [140]; convert to a mark out of [40]. Total : [40]

3

(a) his brother (1) not himself (1) was leader (1) of the citizens (1) of the new city (1) [5]
(b) B [1]
(c) A,D,E [3]
(d) (i) *minimi* (1) very (1) small (1) [3]
(ii) facile / facility / faculty / etc. [1]
(iii) jump over the walls [1]
(e) (i) angry [1]
(ii) he saw (1) his brother (1) jumping over the walls (1) [3]
(iii) killed him (1) at once (1) [2]
(f) he alone (1) had (1) power (1) [3]
(g) (i) called (1) the city (1) Rome / Roma (1) [3]
(ii) they were (1) loyal (1) to Romulus (1) [3]
(h) (i) a few (1) years (1) [2]
(ii) (it was) more (1) powerful (1) than all (1) others (1) [4]

Total [35]

9

1

(a) leader (1) of the city (1) <new> (1) [3]
(b) A,C,F [3]
(c) opened (1) a refuge (1) [2]
(d) many (1) men / people (1) fled there (1) from neighbouring cities (1) [4]
(e) (many were) slaves (1) who had escaped (1) from their masters (1) (others were) wicked men (1) who had stolen (money) (1) or killed (people) (1) [6]

(f) C [1]
(g) no (1) women (1) [2]
(h) how to persuade (1) women (1) to come (1) to the city (1) [4]

Total [25]

2

1 1 1 1 1 11 1 1 1 1 11 1 1 [15]
There were now many men in the city of Rome, but no women.

1 1 11 1 1 1 11 1 1 [11]
Romulus therefore sent messengers to all the *neighbouring* cities,

1 1 1 1 1 1 1 1 [8]
to *invite* the citizens to *Rome* to_a great *show*.

1 1 1 1 1 1 1 1 1 1 1 1 [11]
Very many *families* from *many cities* made a journey *to Rome*,

1 11 1 1 1 1 1 11 1 [11]
to see not only *the show* but also *the* new *city*.

1 1 1 1 1 11 1 11 1 1 [12]
The Romans gladly received them into their houses.

1 1 1 1 1 1 1 1 1 1 [10]
When they saw the *new* forum and *all* the temples,

1 1 1 1 1 1 1 [7]
they were *astonished*, because *the city* had *grown* so quickly.

1 1 1 1 1 1 1 1 1 1 1 1 1 1 [13]
When they *were all* ready to watch *the show*, *Romulus* gave a sign.

1 1 1 1 11 1 [7]
Suddenly the *Roman* young men ran to_*the familes*.

1 1 1 1 1 1 11 1 [9]
They seized *all the maidens and* carried *them* to_their *houses*,

11 1 1 1 [5]
who had come *to Rome* with_*their parents*.

1 1 1 11 11 1 1 1 1 1 1 11 [15]
Their *parents*, who had no *weapons* with them, departed very sad(ly).

1 1 1 1 1 1 [6]
The *Roman young men* now *had* wives.

Total mark = [140]; convert to a mark out of [40]. Total : [40]

3

(a) (i) the Romans (1) had stolen them (1) [2]
(ii) angry [1]
(iii) they persuaded (1) the leaders (1) of their cities (1) to attack (1) Rome (1) [5]
(b) the Romans (1) won (1) [2]
(c) (i) *laetiores* (1) more (1) happy (1) [3]
(ii) they had been seized (1) cruelly (1) [2]
(iii) their husbands (1) had given them (1) love (1) gifts (1) and beautiful homes (1) [5]
(d) (i) B,C,F,H [4]
(ii) marital [1]
(e) A [1]
(f) (i) the wives [1]
(ii) the Romans / their husbands (1) their parents (1) [2]
(iii) turn their swords (1) against them / the wives (1) [2]
(g) they would rather die (1) than live without husbands (1) or parents (1) (accept less precise answers) [3]
(h) peace [1]

Total [35]

10

1

(a) king of Clusium [1]
(b) (i) the Etruscans (1) had built it (1) many years before (1) [3]
(ii) (it had) great (1) power (1) [2]
(c) A,C,F,G [4]
(d) (i) Tarquinius [1]
(ii) fight together [1]
(iii) they are both Etruscan [1]
(e) (i) he feared (1) the growing power (1) of Rome (1) [3]
(ii) *libenter* (1) willingly / gladly (1) [2]
(f) he led (1) a large army (1) into Roman land (1) [3]
(g) (i) he terrified (1) the Romans (1) [2]
(ii) his reputation (1) was (so) great (1) [2]

Total [25]

2

1 1 1 1 1 1 [6]
When *Porsenna* was approaching Rome,

11 1 1 1 1 11 1 1 1 [11]
all the Roman citizens fled from_*the fields* into the city.

1 1 1 1 1 1 1 1 1 11 [11]
Although *Porsenna* attacked *the city* violently, he could not enter,

1 11 1 1 1 1 1 1 1 1 [11]
because part of *the city* was *defended* by walls, *part* by the river.

1 1 1 11 1 [6]
But there was one *bridge*,

1 1 1 1 11 1 1 1 1 1 1 1 [13]
which could give the enemy a way to the middle of *the city*.

1 1 1 1 1 1 1 1 [8]
A few *Roman* soldiers were *guarding* this *bridge*;

1 1 1 1 [4]
As soon as they caught sight of *the enemy*

1 1 1 1 1 1 1 [7]
running from_*the fields* to_*the bridge*, they began to *flee*.

1 1 11 1 1 1 1 1 1 1 1 11 [14]
Horatius however, who by chance was there, begged them to stay.

1 1 1 1 1 1 1 11 1 1 11 1 [14]
'If you wish,' he said, 'to see all *the enemy* in_*the middle of* our *city*,

1 1 1 1 1 1 1 1 1 1 1 [11]
flee; *but if* you want *freedom*, *stay* with me and destroy *the bridge*.

1 1 1 1 11 1 1 1 1 [10]
The Romans, defeated by these words, *began* to *destroy the bridge*

1 1 1 1 [4]
with swords *and* hands.

1 1 1 1 1 1 1 1 1 1 [10]
Meanwhile *Horatius* stood alone on_*the bridge*, waiting for *the enemy*.

Total mark = [140]; convert to a mark out of [40]. Total : [40]

3
(a) *diu* (1) (for) a long time (1) [2]
(b) B [1]
(c) Porsenna (1) could not (1) cross (1) the river (1) [4]
(d) he began to besiege (1) the city (1) [2]
(e) (i) B,C,F [3]
(ii) multitude / multiply / etc. [1]
(f) (i) C [1]
(ii) he didn't know (1) who was (1) the king (1) [3]
(iii) he killed (1) the wrong man / the secretary (1) [2]
(g) he ordered (1) his soldiers (1) to capture / kill (1) the young man (1) [4]
(h) (i) kill him [1]
(ii) many (1) other (1) young men (1) of Rome (1) want (1) to kill him (1) [6]
(i) (i) *perterritus* [1]
(ii) he withdrew (1) his troops (1) from the city (1) [3]
(iii) attack Rome [1]
Total [35]

Section 6: Tests for WJEC Level 2 Additional and GCSE Higher Tier

These are two-part tests. In each test the first part is for comprehension, and the second for translation. The comprehension questions, being very similar to those of previous sections, should be marked in the same way, with due regard for alternative answers. The translations should be marked in two different ways, according to which specification the students are working towards. The mark schemes used here are the more detailed ones used by WJEC, for the reason that these are more difficult for teachers to produce on their own.

Under the WJEC markscheme, all these tests are marked out of 110. Since the number of glossed or repeated words varies from test to test, it sometimes happens that a different raw total would be more appropriate (Test 2, for example, ideally would have a total of at least 125.) However, the same raw total has been retained for all, because then the scaling will be the same for all tests, and so for all candidates from year to year. (The greater the scaling, the less the differentiation.) As a result of this standardisation, it occasionally happens that an inflected word or a proper name loses a mark.

Teachers preparing students for the OCR examination should mark the translations in the same way as in Sections 3 and 4, but dividing the passage into ten more or less equal sections, rather than 5, to give a total out of 40. The mark descriptors are the same, viz.

- [4] Perfectly accurate
- [3] Overall sense correct; minor error(s) (e.g. tense, number)
- [2] Part correct, overall sense lacking / unclear
- [1] Not coherent; isolated knowledge of vocabulary only
- [0] Totally incorrect or omitted.

1

1

(a) Roman (1) senator (1) he (had) wanted for a long time (1)
to be consul (1) [4]

(b) (i) the Roman citizens chose (1) Cicero as consul (1) [2]
(ii) (it contained) very (1) bad men (1) [2]
(iii) conspire (1) against the senate (1) [2]

(c) A,C,E [3]

(d) they ordered two men (1) to go to Cicero's house (1)
the next morning (1) to kill him (1) [4]

(e) he learned of the plot (1) he defended his house (1)
with armed slaves (1) [3]

Total mark for Question 1: [20]

2

1 1 1 1 1 1 1 [7]
As soon as he *beat off* the attack of the two men,

1 1 1 1 [4]
Cicero hurried to the senate,.

1 1 1 1 1 1 1 [7]
to announce to the senators what had happened.

1 1 1 1 1 1 1 1 1 [9]
In the forum too he said to the assembled citizens

1 1 1 1 1 1 1 1 1 1 [10]
that *Catilina* desired his death and that of other *senator*s.

1 1 1 1 1 1 1 1 1 1 [10]
Both the *citizen*s *and* the *senator*s urged him to conquer *the conspirator*s.

1 1 1 1 1 1 1 1 1 [9]
Catilina, having abandoned the city, hurried to *his* army.

1 1 1 1 1 1 1 1 [8]
When someone handed *Cicero* letters,

1 1 1 1 1 [5]
written by the leaders of *the conspiracy*,

1 1 1 1 1 1 1 1 1 [9]
he now had enough *evidence* to seize the leaders.

1 1 1 1 1 1 11 1 1 [10]
He asked *the senators* what he should do about them.

1 1 1 1 1 1 1 1 1 [9]
Some shouted that they should be thrown in(to)_prison,

1 1 1 1 1 [5]
others that they should be killed.

1 1 1 1 1 1 1 1 [8]
At last *Cicero* reluctantly ordered them to be killed.

Total mark = [110]; convert to a mark out of [30]. Total : [30]

2

1

(a) (i) having dinner [1]
(ii) A,D,E [3]
(iii) she was carrying a golden apple (1)
she had not been invited (1) [2]
(b) the most beautiful (1) goddess (1) [2]
(c) (i) departed (1) at once (1) [2]
(ii) began (1) to fight (1) [2]
(iii) all (1) wanted the apple (1) [2]
(d) don't (1) fight (1) [2]
(e) they will have a contest (1) the judge will be Paris (1)
the son of the king of Troy (1)
he is very handsome / we gods favour him (1) [4]

Total mark for Question 1: [20]

2

1 1 1 1 1 1 1 1 1 1 [10]
Jupiter sent *Mercury* to announce to *Paris* what must be done.

1 1 1 1 1 1 [6]
As soon as he heard the words of *Mercury*,

1 1 1 1 1 [5]
Paris caught sight of three goddesses.

1 1 11 1 1 1 1 1 [9]
Since they were all very beautiful, *Paris* was afraid

1 11 1 1 1 1 1 [8]
that the two defeated (goddesses) would punish him.

1 1 1 1 1 1 1 1 [8]
While he was looking at them, *Juno* first said to him:

1 1 1 1 1 1 1 1 1 1 1 [11]
'If you choose me, I will give you a great kingdom.'

1 1 1 1 1 1 [6]
Then *Minerva* promised (that) she would *give* him

1 1 1 1 1 [5]
very *great courage* in war.

1 1 1 1 1 [5]
Finally Venus said, 'Just as you will *choose* me

1 1 1 1 1 1 1 [7]
as the most *beautiful goddess*, you will have a wife,

1 1 1 1 1 1 1 1 1 1 [10]
who is far more *beautiful* than all other women.'

1 1 1 1 1 [5]
After hearing this *Paris chose Venus*.

1 1 1 1 1 1 1 1 [8]
She urged him to make a journey to *Sparta*;

1 1 11 1 1 1 [7]
for there lived *Helen*, the *most beautiful* of *all women*.

Total mark = [110]; convert to a mark out of [30]. Total : [30]

3

1
(a) preparing (1) great games (1) in the circus (1) [3]
(b) A,D,E,H [4]
(c) (i) the games were sacred (1) to the gods (1) [2]
(ii) begged (1) the gods (1) not to be angry (1) [3]
(d) begging the gods [1]
(e) (i) a few (1) days later (1) [2]
(ii) a well-known citizen [1]

(iii) Jupiter appeared (1) to say (1) the games (1)
had not pleased him (1) [4]

Total mark for Question 1: [20]

2

11 1 1 1 1 1 1 1 1 1 1 1 [13]
'Go to the senators,' said *Jupiter*, 'announce these words to them:

1 1 11 1 1 11 1 1 1 1 111 1 1 [17]
the gods are angry. New *games* must be prepared, greater than before.

1 1 1 1 1 1 1 1 1 [9]
Unless they do this, the city will be punished.'

1 1 1 1 1 1 1 1 [8]
Next day, although he wanted to announce to the senators

1 1 1 1 1 1 1 1 1 [9]
that which he had heard, *Latinius* feared they would *laugh at* him.

1 1 1 1 1 1 1 1 1 1 1 1 11 [13]
He therefore stayed at home. That night his son suddenly died.

1 1 1 1 1 1 1 1 1 1 [10]
Latinius, having seen the same *god* again in_*a dream*, still *hesitated*.

1 1 1 1 1 1 1 [7]
Soon he himself was suffering a dreadful *illness*.

1 1 1 1 1 1 1 1 [8]
At last scarcely alive he was carried to the senate.

1 1 1 1 1 1 1 [7]
There he urged *the senators* to *prepare the games again*.

1 1 1 1 1 1 1 1 1 [9]
As soon as they agreed, *Latinius* walked *home* very happy.

Total mark = [110]; convert to a mark out of [30]. Total : [30]

4

1

(a) attacking (1) Corioli (1) [2]

(b) soldier (1) young man (1) [2]

(c) (i) Corioli [1]
(ii) came out (1) of the (gates of) the city (1) [2]
(iii) to attack the Romans [1]
(iv) they were beaten back [1]
(v) B,C,E,G [4]
(d) (i) shouted out [1]
(ii) the rest of the Romans (1) hurried (1) into the city (1) [3]
(e) (i) it was captured [1]
(ii) they named him (1) Coriolanus (1) [2]

Total mark for Question 1: [20]

2

1 1 1 1 1 1 1 1 1 1 [10]
A few years later there was *a shortage* of corn at_Rome.

1 1 1 1 11 1 1 1 [9]
Many senators, first among whom was *Coriolanus*,

1 1 1 1 1 1 [6]
refused to give *corn* to_the lower classes.

1 1 1 1 1 1 1 1 1 1 [10]
The citizens were so angry that they *drove Coriolanus* from the city.

1 1 1 1 1 1 1 [7]
He, after he fled to_*the Volsci*, persuaded them

1 1 1 1 [4]
to *declare war* on the Romans.

1 1 1 1 1 1 1 1 1 [9]
With *Coriolanus* as leader, they often defeated the *Roman* forces.

1 1 1 1 1 1 1 1 [8]
At last, with *many* other *cities* captured,

1 1 1 1 1 1 1 1 1 [9]
the army of *the Volsci* reached the gates of *Rome* itself.

1 1 1 1 1 1 1 [7]
With *the citizens* despairing, the wife *and* mother of *Coriolanus*

1 1 1 1 1 1 1 1 1 [9]
with two sons hurried to the enemy camp.

1 1 1 1 1 1 1 [7]
Before *Coriolanus* could *embrace* them, *his mother* asked him

1 1 1 1 1 1 1 [7]
whether she had come to a son or (to) *an enemy*.

1 1 1 1 11 1 1 [8]
Defeated by these words, *Coriolanus* led *his army* away from_*the city*.

Total mark = [110]; convert to a mark out of [30]. Total : [30]

5

1
(a) (i) waging (1) a long (1) war (1) against neighbouring tribes (1) [4]
(ii) they wanted (1) to conquer (1) Rome (1) [3]
(b) B,D,E [3]
(c) (i) there were so many (1) enemies (1) [2]
(ii) consul [1]
(d) (i) B [1]
(ii) an army (1) against the Veii (1) [2]
(iii) prepare (1) other forces (1) agains the other enemies (1) [3]
(e) when they learned this [1]
Total mark for Question 1: [20]

2
1 1 1 1 [4]
Next day *three hundred and* six *Fabii* marched

1 1 1 1 1 11 1 1 1 1 [11]
through the city streets full of rejoicing citizens.

1 1 1 1 1 1 1 [7]
Having set out from_*the city* with the consul as leader,

1 1 1 1 1 1 1 1 1 1 1 [11]
they came to a wide river. A camp having been placed here,

1 1 1 1 1 1 1 1 1 1 1 [11]
for many days *the Fabii* made attacks upon the territory of_*the Veians*,

1 1 1 1 1 1 1 1 [8]
and even killed some men.

1 1 1 11 11 [7]
At last *the Veians* adopted a new plan:

1 1 1 1 1 1 1 [7]
They led *cattle* into the fields near_*the camp* of *the Fabii*,

1 1 1 1 1 1 1 [7]
so that they would try to capture them.

1 1 1 1 1 1 1 1 1 1 [10]
Soon *the Fabii* were so bold that they advanced far from_*the camp*.

1 1 1 1 1 [5]
Then *the Veians* prepared an ambush:

1 1 1 1 1 1 1 1 1 [9]
suddenly *many* thousands of soldiers *from all sides* attacked *the Fabii*

1 1 1 1 [4]
(as they were) following *the cattle* through_*the fields*.

1 1 1 1 1 1 11 1 [9]
Although they resisted very bravely, *the Fabii* were all killed.

Total mark = [110]; convert to a mark out of [30]. Total : [30]

6

1

(a) (i) king (1) of the gods (1) [2]
(ii) created men / humans [1]
(iii) he wanted (1) (to receive) sacrifices from them(1) [2]
(b) C [1]
(c) (i) when they made (1) the first sacrifice (1) [2]
(ii) to give (1) the gods (1) the bones of the victim (1) wrapped in fat (1) [4]
(d) the men (could) eat the meat / best part (1)
the gods got the poorest part of the animal (*vel sim.*) (1) [2]
(e) A,C,F [3]
(f) (i) Jupiter created (1) women (1) [2]
(ii) because it is the males that will be punished (*vel sim.*) [1]

Total mark for Question 1: [20]

2

1 1 11 1 1 1 [7]
Prometheus was sad, because without fire

1 1 1 1 1 1 1 11 [9]
people had a very miserable life.

1 1 1 1 1 1 [6]
Jupiter however, who had learned that *Prometheus*

1 1 1 1 1 1 1 1 1 1 1 1 1 11 [15]
wished to help *mankind* again, ordered him not to give them fire.

1 1 1 1 1 1 1 1 1 1 [10]
Although he feared the anger of *Jupiter*, *Prometheus gave men fire*,

1 1 1 1 1 11 1 1 1 1 1 1 1 [14]
with which they could *cook* food. They were now much happier.

1 1 1 1 1 1 1 [7]
However, as soon as he realised what *Prometheus* had done,

1 1 1 1 1 1 1 1 1 1 1 [11]
Jupiter was so angry that he decided to punish him.

1 1 1 1 1 1 1 [7]
Captured and taken into the mountains,

1 1 [2]
Prometheus was *tied* to_a *rock*.

1 1 1 1 1 1 [6]
Every day his liver was eaten by a huge *eagle*;

1 1 1 [3]
at night the liver was repaired.

1 1 1 1 1 1 1 1 1 1 1 1 1 [13]
Thus, because he had been kind, he was punished for very many years.

Total mark = [110]; convert to a mark out of [30]. Total : [30]

7

1

(a) (i) C [1]

(ii) friends (1) dogs (1) [2]

(b) (i) they killed (1) many stags (1) [2]

(ii) to carry the (dead) stags (1) home (1) [2]

(c) (i) to walk (1) for longer (1) through the wood (1) with his dogs (1) [4]

(ii) midday (approx.) [1]

(d) (i) a few (1) hours (1) [2]

(ii) A,C,E,H [4]

(e) (i) the woman [1]

(ii) she was naked [1]

Total mark for Question 1: [20]

2

1 1 1 1 1 1 1 1 1 [9]
The woman, whom *Actaeon* had seen, was the goddess *Diana*,

1 1 1 1 1 1 1 1 [8]
who, worn out by *the hunt*, was accustomed to go

1 1 1 1 [4]
every day with her maidservants into_*cave* <that>.

1 1 1 1 1 1 1 1 1 1 1 1 [12]
They, as soon as they *saw* the man, hurried to cover their mistress;

1 1 1 1 1 1 1 1 1 1 1 1 1 1 1 [15]
she, desiring to punish him, had nothing other than water to throw.

1 1 1 1 1 1 1 1 [8]
*throw*ing this in the young man's face, she *curse*d him.

1 1 1 1 1 1 1 1 1 [9]
'Now,' she said, 'you will try to announce to everyone

1 1 1 1 1 1 1 1 1 [9]
that you have seen *a goddess* without clothes – if you can!

1 1 1 1 1 1 1 1 1 1 [10]
Surely_not you will dare to return to your dogs now like this?'

11 1 1 1 1 1 1 1 1 11 [12]
Actaeon felt *a stag*'s *horns grow* on his head. Soon he *had* four feet.

1 1 1 1 1 1 1 1 1 [9]
he ran terrified out of_*the cave*, more quickly than before.

1 1 1 1 1 [5]
At once he was killed by his (own) *dogs*.

Total mark = [110]; convert to a mark out of [30]. Total : [30]

8

1

(a) brave (1) fierce (1) [2]
(b) he was taught (1) to fight (1) with sword (1) (and) spear (1) [4]
(c) A,D,E [3]
(d) (i) escape [1]
(ii) they followed him [1]
(e) (i) *liberatorum* (1) freed (1) [2]
(ii) through the fields (1) <surrounding> (1) [2]
(f) in every place (1) he tried (1) to persuade slaves (1)
to leave their masters (1) [4]
(g) B [1]

Total mark for Question 1: [20]

2

1 1 1 1 1 1 1 1 1 1 1 [11]
After he began to call slaves to_him, in a short time

11 1 1 1 1 1 1 1 1 1 [11]
Spartacus had a large crowd of men and women round_him.

11 1 1 1 1 1 1 1 1 1 [11]
Most of these had never held either a sword or a spear.

1 1 1 1 1 1 1 1 1 [9]
Since he feared that the Romans might send an army against_him,

1 1 1 1 1 1 11 1 1 1 [11]
Spartacus ordered his friends to teach all *the slaves* to fight.

1 1 1 1 1 1 1 11 1 1 1 [12]
At the same *time* those_who could made new *swords* and *spears*.

1 1 1 1 1 1 1 1 1 1 [10]
Soon so great *an army* of *armed men* was ready to *fight* for_*freedom*,

1 11 1 1 1 1 1 1 1 [10]
that the first *army*, which *the Romans sent*, was easily defeated.

1 1 1 1 1 1 1 1 1 [9]
Then however another *and larger Roman_army* arrived,

11 1 1 1 1 [6]
led by a more *experienced* general.

1 1 1 1 1 1 1 1 1 1 [10]
This_*army* defeated the forces of *Spartacus*; he himself was killed.

Total mark = [110]; convert to a mark out of [30]. Total : [30]

9

1

(a) he loved (1) many (1) women (1) [3]
(b) A,E,F,H [4]
(c) (i) his sister [1]
(ii) after (1) she died (1) he gave her (1) the greatest honours (1) [4]
(d) for a long time (1) she received (1) the love (1) of the emperor (1) [4]
(e) she wasn't beautiful (1) or young (1)
she had three daughters (1) from another man (1) [4]

Total mark for Question 1: [20]

2

1 1 1 1 1 1 1 1 [8]
Through(out) the four years in_which he held power,

1 1 1 11 1 1 1 1 1 [10]
Caligula killed so many men that the citizens greatly feared,

1 1 1 1 1 1 1 1 [8]
lest the anger of the emperor be turned against_them.

1 1 1 1 1 1 1 1 [8]
He killed many to seize their money,

1 1 1 1 1 1 1 1 [8]
others because they had not praised him enough,

1 1 1 1 1 1 1 1 1 1 1 11 [13]
the rest for no other reason than because they were excellent men.

1 1 1 1 1 1 1 [7]
The senators, who hated him (very) greatly,

1 1 1 1 1 1 1 1 1 1 [10]
at last persuaded two soldiers to_*strike the emperor* with swords.

1 1 1 [3]
While they were *killing the emperor*,

1 1 1 1 1 1 1 1 1 [9]
the soldiers saw an old man hidden behind a door.

1 1 1 1 1 1 [6]
Because he had seen what had happened,

1 1 1 1 1 [5]
they prepared to *kill* him too.

1 1 1 1 [4]
Then *the soldiers recognised the old man*:

1 1 1 [3]
it was *Claudius*, *Caligula*'s *uncle*.

1 1 1 1 1 1 1 1 [8]
The soldiers announced at once that he would be *the next_emperor*.

Total mark = [110]; convert to a mark out of [30]. Total : [30]

10

1

(a) the daughter (1) of a poor man (1) [2]
(b) (i) she had great skill (1) at spinning (and weaving) (1) [2]
(ii) C [1]
(c) (i) that she had been taught (1) by Minerva (1) [2]
(ii) it was very great [1]
(d) A,C,F [3]
(e) her skill (1) was much better (1) than Minerva's (1) [3]
(f) (i) that Minerva (1) would have a contest (with her) (1) [2]
(ii) (the speaker) would (soon) understand (1)
that Minerva had much to learn from her (1)
(Allow 1 for 'she thought she would win'.) [2]

(g) (i) very angry [1]

(ii) Arachne should be punished [1]

Total mark for Question 1: [20]

2

1 1 1 1 1 [5]

Minerva was wearing the clothes *of an old woman.*

1 1 1 1 1 1 1 1 1 [9]

Having entered *Arachne*'s house, she spoke slowly like *an old woman.*

1 1 1 1 1 1 [6]

'You must accept my advice.

1 1 1 1 1 1 1 1 [8]

If you ask for *the forgiveness* of the goddess for your words,

1 1 1 1 [4]

she will give *forgiveness.*'

11 1 1 1 1 1 1 1 1 1 1 1 [13]

Arachne said, 'Do you dare to come to_me thus worn out by years?

1 1 1 1 1 1 1 1 1 [9]

Your stupid words will never persuade me.

1 1 1 1 1 1 1 [7]

Why does *the goddess* herself not come to *have a contest*?'

1 1 1 1 1 1 1 1 [8]

Minerva, having *changed* her clothes, at once replied: 'I have come!'

1 1 1 1 11 1 [7]

Both the woman *and the goddess* sat at_*the looms.*

1 1 1 [3]

They began to *weave.*

1 1 1 1 1 1 1 1 1 1 [10]

After many hours they inspected the finished *tapestries*:

1 1 1 1 1 [5]

both were equally beautiful.

1 1 1 1 1 1 1 1 1 [9]

The goddess was so angry that she *changed Arachne* into_*a spider.*

1 1 1 1 1 1 1 [7]
'*Thus* you will always be able *to weave*,' she said laughing.

Total mark = [110]; convert to a mark out of [30]. Total : [30]

Appendix 1: Scaling chart for 150 → 50 (for Section 2)

150	50	**115**	38	**80**	27	**45**	15	**10**	3
149	50	**114**	38	**79**	26	**44**	15	**9**	3
148	49	**113**	38	**78**	26	**43**	14	**8**	3
147	49	**112**	37	**77**	26	**42**	14	**7**	2
146	49	**111**	37	**76**	25	**41**	14	**6**	2
145	48	**110**	37	**75**	25	**40**	13	**5**	2
144	48	**109**	36	**74**	25	**39**	13	**4**	1
143	48	**108**	36	**73**	24	**38**	13	**3**	1
142	47	**107**	36	**72**	24	**37**	12	**2**	1
141	47	**106**	35	**71**	24	**36**	12	**1**	0
140	47	**105**	35	**70**	23	**35**	12		
139	46	**104**	35	**69**	23	**34**	11		
138	46	**103**	34	**68**	23	**33**	11		
137	46	**102**	34	**67**	22	**32**	11		
136	45	**101**	34	**66**	22	**31**	10		
135	45	**100**	33	**65**	22	**30**	10		
134	45	**99**	33	**64**	21	**29**	10		
133	44	**98**	33	**63**	21	**28**	9		
132	44	**97**	32	**62**	21	**27**	9		
131	44	**96**	32	**61**	20	**26**	9		
130	43	**95**	32	**60**	20	**25**	8		
129	43	**94**	31	**59**	20	**24**	8		
128	43	**93**	31	**58**	19	**23**	8		
127	42	**92**	31	**57**	19	**22**	7		
126	42	**91**	30	**56**	19	**21**	7		
125	42	**90**	30	**55**	18	**20**	7		
124	41	**89**	30	**54**	18	**19**	6		
123	41	**88**	29	**53**	18	**18**	6		
122	41	**87**	29	**52**	17	**17**	6		
121	40	**86**	29	**51**	17	**16**	5		
120	40	**85**	28	**50**	17	**15**	5		
119	40	**84**	28	**49**	16	**14**	5		
118	39	**83**	28	**48**	16	**13**	4		
117	39	**82**	27	**47**	16	**12**	4		
116	39	**81**	27	**46**	15	**11**	4		

Appendix 2: Scaling chart for 140 → 40 (for Section 5)

140	40	**105**	30	**70**	20	**35**	10
139	40	**104**	30	**69**	20	**34**	10
138	39	**103**	29	**68**	19	**33**	9
137	39	**102**	29	**67**	19	**32**	9
136	39	**101**	29	**66**	19	**31**	9
135	39	**100**	29	**65**	19	**30**	9
134	38	**99**	28	**64**	18	**29**	8
133	38	**98**	28	**63**	18	**28**	8
132	38	**97**	28	**62**	18	**27**	8
131	37	**96**	27	**61**	17	**26**	7
130	37	**95**	27	**60**	17	**25**	7
129	37	**94**	27	**59**	17	**24**	7
128	37	**93**	27	**58**	17	**23**	7
127	36	**92**	26	**57**	16	**22**	6
126	36	**91**	26	**56**	16	**21**	6
125	36	**90**	26	**55**	16	**20**	6
124	35	**89**	25	**54**	15	**19**	5
123	35	**88**	25	**53**	15	**18**	5
122	35	**87**	25	**52**	15	**17**	5
121	35	**86**	25	**51**	15	**16**	5
120	34	**85**	24	**50**	14	**15**	4
119	34	**84**	24	**49**	14	**14**	4
118	34	**83**	24	**48**	14	**13**	4
117	33	**82**	23	**47**	13	**12**	3
116	33	**81**	23	**46**	13	**11**	3
115	33	**80**	23	**45**	13	**10**	3
114	33	**79**	23	**44**	13	**9**	3
113	32	**78**	22	**43**	12	**8**	2
112	32	**77**	22	**42**	12	**7**	2
111	32	**76**	22	**41**	12	**6**	2
110	31	**75**	21	**40**	11	**5**	1
109	31	**74**	21	**39**	11	**4**	1
108	31	**73**	21	**38**	11	**3**	1
107	31	**72**	21	**37**	11	**2**	1
106	30	**71**	20	**36**	10	**1**	0

Appendix 3: Scaling chart for 130 → 40 (for Section 5)

		105	32	**70**	22	**35**	11
		104	32	**69**	21	**34**	10
		103	32	**68**	21	**33**	10
		102	31	**67**	21	**32**	10
		101	31	**66**	20	**31**	10
		100	31	**65**	20	**30**	9
		99	30	**64**	20	**29**	9
		98	30	**63**	19	**28**	9
		97	30	**62**	19	**27**	8
		96	30	**61**	19	**26**	8
130	40	**95**	29	**60**	18	**25**	8
129	40	**94**	29	**59**	18	**24**	7
128	39	**93**	29	**58**	18	**23**	7
127	39	**92**	28	**57**	18	**22**	7
126	39	**91**	28	**56**	17	**21**	6
125	38	**90**	28	**55**	17	**20**	6
124	38	**89**	27	**54**	17	**19**	6
123	38	**88**	27	**53**	16	**18**	6
122	38	**87**	27	**52**	16	**17**	5
121	37	**86**	26	**51**	16	**16**	5
120	37	**85**	26	**50**	15	**15**	5
119	37	**84**	26	**49**	15	**14**	4
118	36	**83**	26	**48**	15	**13**	4
117	36	**82**	25	**47**	14	**12**	4
116	36	**81**	25	**46**	14	**11**	3
115	35	**80**	25	**45**	14	**10**	3
114	35	**79**	24	**44**	14	**9**	3
113	35	**78**	24	**43**	13	**8**	2
112	34	**77**	24	**42**	13	**7**	2
111	34	**76**	23	**41**	13	**6**	2
110	34	**75**	23	**40**	12	**5**	2
109	34	**74**	23	**39**	12	**4**	1
108	33	**73**	22	**38**	12	**3**	1
107	33	**72**	22	**37**	11	**2**	1
106	33	**71**	22	**36**	11	**1**	0

Appendix 4: Scaling chart for 110 → 30 (for Section 6)

110	30	**75**	20	**40**	11	**5**	1
109	30	**74**	20	**39**	11	**4**	1
108	29	**73**	20	**38**	11	**3**	1
107	29	**72**	20	**37**	11	**2**	1
106	29	**71**	19	**36**	10	**1**	0
105	29	**70**	19	**35**	10		
104	28	**69**	19	**34**	10		
103	28	**68**	19	**33**	9		
102	28	**67**	18	**32**	9		
101	28	**66**	18	**31**	9		
100	27	**65**	18	**30**	9		
99	27	**64**	17	**29**	8		
98	27	**63**	17	**28**	8		
97	26	**62**	17	**27**	8		
96	26	**61**	17	**26**	7		
95	26	**60**	16	**25**	7		
94	26	**59**	16	**24**	7		
93	25	**58**	16	**23**	7		
92	25	**57**	16	**22**	6		
91	25	**56**	15	**21**	6		
90	25	**55**	15	**20**	6		
89	24	**54**	15	**19**	5		
88	24	**53**	14	**18**	5		
87	24	**52**	14	**17**	5		
86	23	**51**	14	**16**	5		
85	23	**50**	14	**15**	4		
84	23	**49**	13	**14**	4		
83	23	**48**	13	**13**	4		
82	22	**47**	13	**12**	3		
81	22	**46**	13	**11**	3		
80	22	**45**	12	**10**	3		
79	22	**44**	12	**9**	3		
78	21	**43**	12	**8**	2		
77	21	**42**	11	**7**	2		
76	21	**41**	11	**6**	2		

Printed in Great Britain
by Amazon